POLISHING THE DIAMOND

ENLIGHTENING THE MIND

REFLECTIONS OF A

KOREAN BUDDHIST MASTER

POLISHING THE DIAMOND

◆

ENLIGHTENING THE MIND

Reflections of a
Korean Buddhist Master

Kim Jae Woong

Yong Hwa

Table of Contents

Foreword

Polishing the Diamond, Enlightening the Mind is a book compiled by Kim Jae Woong out of gratitude and devotion for his Korean Buddhist master, Baek Sung Wook. It contains the master's instructions and advice for cultivating the mind in the quest for enlightenment.

Despite wanting happiness and wishing to avoid suffering, human beings constantly engage in activities that give rise to fear, disease, starvation, and ultimately death. Under such circumstances it would be wonderful if even a few people could create some inner peace, if only for a short time. I am confident that readers who seek such a goal will find valuable advice in this book.

Venerable Tenzin Gyatso, the 14th Dalai Lama of Tibet
November 12, 1996

Preface

I have been told that the few books I have written have been of some help to practitioners. Now in my seventies, I began writing again, believing that stories of practice taken from the time of my mid-fifties to the present day could also assist those who cultivate the mind.

Practitioners should not perform deeds, say words, or entertain thoughts that cause them to commit sins. Following the example of the enlightened masters of the past, they should practice many good deeds every day, and not grow lazy in accumulating blessed virtue. The mind's scale should always incline towards incurring blessed virtue rather than committing sins.

I believe one should always practice lowering oneself with humility, practice the mindset of always seeking advice and learning from others, and lead a life that brings benefit to one's surroundings. When meeting others or when approaching a task, one should be sure always to practice restraint, endurance and humbleness, and surrender the mind. Surely, the path of one who cultivates the mind lies in the constant practice of the Bodhisattva's mind, the Bodhisattva's acts, and following the Bodhisattva's path.

I laid the foundations of my practice following Master Baek's method of reading the Diamond Sutra, practicing its teachings, and surrendering the mind. Let us all practice together.

January 2013
Kim Jae Woong

Introduction

The Enlightened Teacher,
Master Baek Sung Wook

STUDYING UNDER THE MASTER

The first time I met Master Baek was in April 1964. I was then twenty-four years old. Since my youth, I have believed that the fate of a nation rests on the education of its people. So, I thought that if we built a special teachers university and produced true teachers, we could better the character and conscience of all Koreans, eradicating our perpetual vices and bad habits. In order to set the foundation for this project, I started a small business. Also, to seek advice, I spent time meeting everyone whom I thought was wise. It was through this project that I met Master Baek.

When Mr. Ra Dong-yeong, a graduate student of Dongguk University, told me that Master Baek was residing in the town of Sosa in Bucheon City, in Gyeonggi Province, I set out to find him. When I arrived there, I said that I had come from Second Eulji Avenue, Seoul, and that I wished to see Master Baek. Mr. Kim Cheol-su, who was attending the master at the time, led me to see him. Containing my excitement, I entered the quiet Buddha hall. Master Baek's presence was as blinding as the bright sunshine.

A hazy and luminous energy surrounded the area where Master Baek sat. With his solemn yet serene expression, he seemed to see straight through my mind. He had the look of an enlightened man who would not even allow a speck of karmic hindrance to remain in those who came before him. The moment I bowed down and sat in front of him, all my inner discriminations quietly settled down.

After a long silence, I stated the purpose of my visit and asked him if there was any way I could swiftly achieve my goal of building the special teachers university. He seemed to gaze at me for a long time, when at last he told me that all I had to do was to follow his instructions. I was glad to hear this, so I quickly asked him, "What would you have me do, sir?"

He said, "I will tell you if you first say that you'll do it."

Since it is my nature to always honor my promises, I could not easily make this promise without some hesitation. A good while passed in silence.

"Will you do as I say or not?"

Silence.

Because there still was no answer from me, we sat quietly for a while. He then patiently asked me again,

"Will you do as I say or not?"

Silence.

He asked me again. "Will you do it or not?"

Behind his three carefully and patiently repeated questions, there seemed to be a bright hope. I felt that the venture might be an auspicious one.

"Yes, I will do it, sir."

"Good. Read the Diamond Sutra both in the morning and in the evening, and surrender any thought that arises in your mind to Buddha by reciting *Mireukjon Yeoraebul* (Tathagata Maitreya—the future Buddha)."

Until then, I thought achieving social projects by reading sutras or by prayer was impossible, so I was very perplexed by his answer. But, as soon as I said, "Yes," my mind was illuminated as if white light had completely filled my heart. I felt a deep happiness. I felt like a lost ship struggling on a dark stormy ocean that had finally come upon a lighthouse.

After that first meeting, I visited Master Baek occasionally at Sosa to ask him questions. Later, I went to see him once a week, so that he could check my progress. Following his teachings, I put great effort into my practice. Even when I was busy running my business and living by myself, I read the sutra nine times a day. And as I gradually changed and expanded my business, I became single-mindedly determined to do a great work for society. During that time, my teacher seemed like such a kind, considerate person, checking every detail of my spiritual practice. His compassionate attention was like a warm spring breeze blowing through my heart, whisking away the dust of my bleak past.

In April 1966, after I had finished supporting my sister in her education, I entered the monastery at Sosa to study more seriously with Master Baek on his recommendation. But from the first day in the monastery, I felt as if I had been totally abandoned by my teacher. He was so strict and cold that I sometimes wondered why I went there in the first place.

Much later I came to understand that Master Baek's cold-heartedness was actually his compassionate way of teaching. As a spiritual seeker who needed to devote all my mind and body to solving the problem of repeated birth and death, I needed to get rid of my dependence on him and develop a strong conviction of my own.

Life at Sosa began at three in the morning, when we rose for our morning practice. At half past four, we listened to our master's Dharma lecture, and Master Baek would check the results of our previous day's practices. During these interviews, we revealed to our master all the intentions, realizations, dreams, and visions that had arisen in our minds, as if we were surrendering them to him. We then learned to cultivate our minds by working on the things that he pointed out.

Going to see my master the morning after a day when I had been unmindful made me feel like a cow being dragged to the slaughter house. Revealing my karmic hindrances in public was as painful as tearing out my own flesh, though this was the only way they would melt away and my mind would be cultivated.

My teacher used to say to us, "Release as many of your flaws as you can in front of me, and be the greatest person you can be outside of this place!" as he gently soothed every one of our karmic hindrances. During all those years, he never once missed checking our practice each morning. Much later, I began to see just how hard his task was.

My teacher perceived things beyond time and space. Two particular instances come to mind.

After seven and a half years of life at Sosa, I moved to Pohang. There I had breakfast at 10 A.M. and dinner at 2:30 P.M., and did not eat afterwards. One day, however, I was too busy to eat dinner on time. I became hungry later, so I ate some bread at 10 P.M. Back then, I used to go to Seoul once a month to visit my master to have my progress checked. When I went up to see him that time, he said to me, "I see that you couldn't even keep the schedule for your two meals a day, and instead you had to eat something around ten at night."

For the first eight months that I was in Pohang, I slept in a sitting position without reclining on anything. When I began to sleep in a sitting position, I found that my body was more refreshed compared to when I slept lying down. Even so, in the summertime, when I saw some people leaning against a tree to sleep in its shade, I felt envious. Then I even became tired of leaning against a wall during sleep and, a couple of days later, I started to sleep lying down. Soon thereafter I went to see my teacher, and somehow he knew that I had been sleeping on the floor, and he scolded me severely for not sleeping in a sitting position. He knew everything that was going on in Pohang from three hundred miles away in Seoul. Probably nothing in this world is harder than attending a master who can see through your mind.

Once, when I was at Sosa, Master Baek had to go to Seoul. When he came back that night, he said that he was sorry he could not look after us when we needed him during the day. While living in the same place as us, he checked our mental state many times each day. He came to encourage the ones whose minds were faltering, and he always came to make a confirmation the moment Dharma awakened in one of us.

Among our daily tasks at Sosa Monastery, the first chore of the day was milking the cows, of whom we had as many as fifteen at one point. The task of feeding, cleaning, and grazing the cows was itself overwhelming. On top of this, we did everything from cultivating fields to clearing waste lands. Our schedule was full of busy labor without rest.

One experience of milking the cows in the summer is still fresh in my memory. It was so hot and muggy that, even sitting still, I was bathed in sweat. Milking a cow on a day like that, with my right shoulder and face pressed against the cow's steamy leg and stomach, was unbearable. The worst times were when the cow would hit my mouth and eyes with her manure-caked tail as she tried to chase away the flies. What sickening moments those were! Nevertheless, I was truly grateful for the Dharma-hitting of the cow's tail, since the quick and intense surrender of my nauseating disgust helped me become awakened to so much wisdom. At those moments, the cow's tail was my teacher, enlightening my mind.

Once, I overheard my teacher mention to someone that the reason he had started a farm was to help spiritual seekers plant merit and to help their spiritual practice. While working on the farm and practicing our master's teaching, we came to realize that our labor and spiritual practice were not two different things. Also, while conditioning our consciousness to "work to feed others," we believed that everything we did, from eating to breathing, was a continuation of our efforts to serve Buddha well.

Sentient beings' attachments to their bodies are embedded in sleeping, eating, and being comfortable. The practices we did, such as eating only two meals a day without any snack, continuously planting merit through hard work, and continuing to practice throughout the night, were all designed to stimulate our egos and our attachments to our bodies so that we could then surrender the attached states of mind that arose in such conditions. Karmic hindrances have to be cleansed from the mind the moment they arise; otherwise you lose your chance.

Cultivating my mind was as painful as carving out my bones. Our master's Dharma-hitting fiercely struck down on us every time we lost our mindfulness. The harsher the conditions, I suppose, the more pure and fragrant must the lotus flower blossom. This constant practice of surrendering my disdain for hard work, surrendering my attachments to eating and sleeping, surrendering the temptation to run away from the monastery, surrendering my karmic hindrances, and even surrendering the Buddha that I revered—all this made me truly understand, to the marrow of my bones, my teacher's goal when he first built the monastery: to raise Buddhas.

The place where I sacrificed life's most precious youth and all my destiny to serve Buddha, the place where I offered the highest reverence, the place where I devoted myself to spiritual practice with the agony of crossing the line of life and death so many times a day—these memories of the monastery, along with my master's loving smile, have become part of the past that will never return. It is difficult for me to hide my sadness and longing, but I also surrender these feelings to Buddha according to his teaching.

Cultivating your mind means curing your inner problems— wrong habits ingrained in you that give rise to wrongful acts. You cultivate the mind when you confront each crucial moment, each karmic hindrance, from your past lives. While I was trying so hard on my own to rid myself of bad habits, habits to which I had been conditioned over many past lives, my master helped me by hitting my karmic hindrances with his fist.

Once, my face turned bright red from his Dharma-hitting. And if it hurt someone as young as me so much, how painful it must have been for an old man like him, who at the time was close to eighty years old! Why was he going through so much trouble to teach an impossible person like me? I was so deeply moved by his compassion that I bowed down on the ground to him three times and cried my heart out.

FOLLOWING IN THE FOOTSTEPS
OF THE MASTER

Master Baek was born on the nineteenth day of the eighth lunar month in the year 1897 in Seoul, Korea. He renounced the world—was ordained as a Buddhist monk—at the age of fourteen, graduated from Gyeongseong Central Buddhist Institute when he was twenty-three, and went to Shanghai to participate in the Korean government-in-exile following the March 1st Korean Independence movement of 1919.

Later, he came to believe that, in order to achieve Korean liberation swiftly, Korean youth must have a modern education. Therefore, he set a goal to awaken, or educate, two hundred thousand young Koreans. In preparation for his project, he left Korea to study in Europe. After graduating from high school in Paris, he earned his Ph.D. in philosophy in 1925 from Würzburg University in southern Germany with a dissertation entitled *Buddhist Metaphysics*, after which he returned to Korea.

He was a professor at the Central Buddhist Professional Institute for three years. However, because he was under strict surveillance by the Japanese police as a subversive character, and because the social conditions were not favorable at the time, he could not fulfill his earlier dream of educating two hundred thousand Korean youths. Prevented from achieving his goal, he retired from worldly life and entered the retreat at Geumgang Mountain in 1928. His reasons for entering the mountain retreat could only have been for the liberation of

Korea and for leading all beings to salvation.

A little while after he started his practice at the mountain, he became aware of the future of Korea and was assured of her liberation. He then thought about changing his body—passing on to the next life—because he had no more attachment to this world. However, looking further into the future, he saw that he still had tasks left at Sosa Monastery. Thus, he decided to continue his life.

He became enlightened while studying at Anyang-am and Jijang-am at Geumgang Mountain for ten years, and he taught many students at Jijang-am. In 1938, because of pressure from the Japanese police, he ended his practice among his students and returned home to practice alone in Seoul.

After Korean independence, Master Baek participated in establishing the Korean government. In 1950, he was inaugurated as Minister of Home Affairs and was active in setting the foundation of the country. Later he was in charge of the Public Corporation of Mining Promotion. With his wisdom-eye that could see sixteen-feet underground, he found many tungsten deposits and thus gave some breathing room to the country's faltering economy.

In 1953, he became the president of Dongguk University, and during those hard social and economic times, he established the basis for today's Dongguk University. Furthermore, he pushed forward with many of his plans to make the university a world-class institution, though he did not get to see those plans come to fruition. Master Baek later commented on his attempt to raise Dongguk University's standard. He said that, since the people who were potentially at the receiving end of good fortune (the students of Dongguk University) lacked merit, even if someone wanted to provide them good fortune, the karma was not there for them to receive it.

In 1962, he retired from all of his social responsibilities and built a little monastery at the foot of Sosa's green hill. He became fully enlightened while residing there, and he immersed himself in enlightening the human nature of those with deep spiritual roots who came to see him. At the place where a carving of the Diamond Sutra passage "Thus ye shall view" hung instead of a doorplate, there remained the full radiance of my master's later years, along with the fierce efforts of other spiritual seekers.

According to his teaching "set your goal to Mahayana, but live your life as a Hinayana practitioner," Master Baek's daily life never deviated at all from the proper life of a spiritual seeker. Since the time he entered the mountain retreat at the age of thirty-one, he always rose at the hour of the tiger (between 3 A.M. and 5 A.M.) to wash and begin his practice. He was so strict that he did not eat his meals if it were even five minutes past meal time, or "offering time," in the monastery.

Even while he was in public service, he never came out of his place of practice after 6 P.M. When he held the presidency at Dongguk University, he worked from early in the morning and came back to his place to practice in the afternoon after 3 o' clock.

Until he was over eighty years old, he always changed the briquette in his room and cleaned the ashes by himself, and he never let anyone do his laundry. Even when his students tried to take care of his chores, he always refused them and did them himself.

On the nineteenth day of the eighth lunar month in 1981, on the same month and the same day he was born, he passed away, lying on his side, with a peaceful expression on his face.

ABOUT THE MASTER'S TEACHING

Master Baek always told us a few things during our morning interviews to help lead us to the path of enlightenment and to awaken us from our karmic hindrances. Following are a few quotes taken from these morning interviews.

> Surrender to Buddha the thoughts, impressions, emotions, and ideas that arise in your mind. The practice of surrendering should be done out of the reverence that arises in your mind and not at someone else's request. If you do not surrender your thoughts out of reverence, you get caught up in dualistic thinking. You should surrender constantly. When surrendering is accompanied by reverence, you will attain bright wisdom, and you should put these realizations into practice. When you generate reverence to Buddha, there are no afterthoughts remaining, so there is no attachment to anything. You will realize and become aware of things as you constantly practice surrendering, but do not dwell on how you came to achieve those realizations. When reverence arises in you, you hear the Dharma lecture that completely fills the universe.
>
> In cleansing one's attachment to sleep, do not say, "I am not sleeping." Instead say, "When do I have time to sleep, since I am full of reverence and joy?"

The offering of the *won,* or selfless vow, should be invoked naturally. But, if you say, "natural," you digress from the won.

Surrender even the thought, "I have surrendered my arising thoughts again and again." If you think that you have surrendered many times, all you will have is that notion that you have surrendered many times. The karmic hindrances you have accumulated for many eons will not leave you.

Master Baek always stressed that there should be a way to cultivate the mind that fits the lifestyle of modern people. Spiritual sects usually teach us to let go, cut, or calm our discriminating minds. But our master always said,

When I do not have any power, with what strength can I cut the violent karma and sufferings that hide in and arise from the depth of my mind? If you say, "I" will let go of sufferings and delusions, you are only conditioning your ego. Therefore, surrender your sufferings and karmic retributions to Buddha with reverence.

Master Baek realized the practice of surrendering one's mind within the Diamond Sutra after starting his life at Sosa Monastery. Master Baek himself achieved enlightenment through this method. He once commented on this method, saying,

My level of enlightenment has been different at

different periods in my life. My level at Geumgang Mountain was different, my level at Dongguk University was different, even my level at Sosa has been different from beginning, to middle, to end. You don't know how fortunate you all are. Do you know how tough a time I had before I realized this method of surrendering? Where else can you find people following such an easy path to enlightenment?

When you offer up—surrender—your sufferings to Buddha, you accumulate merit through your offerings, you practice your reverence to Buddha, you free yourself from exchanging negative karma with others, and you can attain enlightenment. So, surrender your arising mind, thought, emotion, and impressions this very moment to Buddha with reverence.

Master Baek also said that the Diamond Sutra embodies the essence of Shakyamuni Buddha's spiritual attainment, for this Dharma lecture was given when his mind and body were at their healthiest. If you compare it to the sun, his enlightenment was shining brilliantly like the sun at noon. This sutra is radiance itself. Therefore, Master Baek also said that if you read the sutra, which is Buddha's enlightenment and radiance, you face his wisdom. By becoming one with his radiance, you free yourself from the shadow of karmic hindrance and misfortune, and enlighten your human nature.

The practices he recommended, including the method of surrendering, are:

While reciting *Mireukjon Yeoraebul* with your mind, hear it through your ears, and practice surrendering all your thoughts to the Buddha. If you hold on to the thoughts in your mind, they will cause you to become ill. If you suppress them, they will explode. Surrendering is the spiritual seeker's "conquest of mind."

Read the Diamond Sutra in the morning and in the evening. Learn it as if you are actually in front of the Buddha, learning directly from him, and make a habit of practicing what you have learned. Let your body work regularly, but keep your mind absolutely still. If you do this for one hundred days and repeat the hundred-day practice about ten times, you will attain the ability to see your past lives and to see others' past lives as well, because your ego will have melted away. This could be called the attainment of beginning Buddhist practice.

You should be cautious of saying, "I am going to devote myself to practice," for that is the mind of greed. If you say, "My practice isn't going well," that is the mind of anger. And if you say, "My practice is going well," that is the mind of ignorant arrogance. Therefore, not doing those three is the practice of the path. Practice diligently, and as long as you do not *not do* your practice, you will be fine. An ancient sage said, "Practice unceasingly, not intensely."

O n e

The World That Is Created
By The Mind

SOUND OF A BELL

Once, when Kang Xi, the second emperor of the Qing Dynasty, was a crown prince, he went to Wu Tai Mountain to meditate. He usually practiced Chan (Zen). One day, as he was taking a walk around the temple grounds, he heard an evening bell toll. Suddenly, the ringing no longer came from the bell, but it peacefully resonated from deep within his mind.

Upon experiencing such a rare phenomenon, he asked one of the courtiers by his side with great delight, "How does that bell sound to you?" A monk standing next to the courtier, who was not even addressed by the prince, abruptly interrupted the conversation to impress him, saying, "My lord, even the sound of a black crow is Buddha's teaching." In that moment, a severe disgust arose in the prince's mind at the way the monk tried to impress him, completely destroying the prince's *samadhi*—the meditative state characterized by calm, stability, and the absence of distraction.

According to Master Baek, hearing the sound of a bell as the sound of one's mind is a hard level to achieve for a spiritual practitioner because it means that one's ego has melted away. He said that if the ringing resembles the sound of the bell and the sound of your mind, your practice is halfway there. If the ringing sounds like it comes entirely from the bell, then you should know that you are just starting on your spiritual path. To test our stages of development, our teacher asked us from time to time where we thought the sounds from outside—such as that of a bell, gong, or carriage—were coming from.

18

THE IMAGE IN THE MIND

In the paintings of Kim Eun-ho, the images of Sin Saimdang (an ideal Korean mother and wife) and Nongae (a patriotic heroine) look similar. Although the appearances of Sin Saimdang and Nongae should be different, the reason that they give out such similar feelings is because there is only one image of a woman that the artist reveres. Even among the portraits of women by many Western artists, we see that each artist does not stray far from a single feeling. This is because there is only one image of a beautiful woman in the mind of every artist.

Just as there are images of ideal women in the minds of artists, when we say we serve Buddha or Jesus, wouldn't our Buddha or Jesus be none other than our mind's image? Since my image is different from everyone else's, such an image is probably only my own idea.

Most of us revere and live with a Buddha or Jesus who is limited by our own imagination and experiences. Isn't this true "idol worship"? To surrender my idea, the idol, is true spiritual practice. When you can surrender your ideas, which are shadows in your mind, only then will you truly perceive Buddha.

Even with religion, Buddha, or the truth—if you enclose them in your mind, they become nonreligion, an idol, and a nontruth. If your mind is tainted by the shadows of "truth" or "religion," your wisdom is tarnished before you even begin. There is a saying that goes, "Do not stay where Buddha is and run away from where there is no Buddha." Surrendering each arising thought is truly the noble thing to do.

A MILLIONAIRE'S KARMIC RETRIBUTION

Once, there was a wealthy American industrialist who, as he was accumulating his wealth, ate less in order to hoard money. Even after he became a tycoon, he cared so much about his money that once, when a public phone did not return his coin, he went all the way to the phone company to get his money back. He changed his mind just before he was about to sign his name on a complaint card.

His stingy habits of not eating and not spending were so severe that eventually his mind became hardened. In his later years, he could no longer eat. He tried all sorts of methods, but still he could not eat. Finally, he announced that he would share a large portion of his wealth with anyone who could feed him for a week.

Then, a doctor came up with a brilliant idea. He told the man to invite one hundred babies to a huge dinner party and to serve those babies himself. The babies, as usual, spilled and dropped their food as they ate. The man couldn't stand to see the food being wasted, so he hastily picked it up and ate it. Since he opened his mind to feed other people, he accumulated merit, and, through his merit, his hungry ghost karma was momentarily calmed.

In order for the millionaire to cure his disease completely, he needed to purify his mentality of eating less to save money, a habit he had been practicing for a long time. If, at seventy years old, he had been practicing this stingy mind since he was twenty, then he would have had fifty years' worth of poison to surrender to Buddha.

When you begin spiritual practice, you regress to your past to purify your mind. Cultivating your mind today will free yesterday's and the day before yesterday's mind. Continuing one more day will cleanse your mind from three days and four days ago. Cultivating your mind for three days will purify your mind from six days ago, seven days ago, and so on.

If the American industrialist had regressed twenty years by practicing in this way, he could have completely cured his illness. It would have been similar to when subconscious problems are cured in psychotherapy. Cultivating one's mind means surrendering not only the diseased aspect of the mind that has been accumulating in one's subconscious, but also surrendering every conditioned human discrimination, leaving no trace, either good or bad.

SURRENDERING YOUR DELUSIONS

Regardless of who you are, if you harbor hatred against others, you will be hated by others, because the being who is closest to your hateful mind is you, your own body and no one else's.

If you respect others, due to your respectful mind you will be respected by others. Looking down on others and trying to be above everyone else will instead put you below everyone else. Thus it is said that if you look down on others, you will be short of stature in your next life. Since the mind that is belittling others is your own, you yourself will appear stunted. One who views others as undesirable will have an undesirable face, while one who respects and looks up to others will have a noble and handsome appearance.

If a human hits an animal such as a cow or a dog, he imprints the animal's image strongly in his own mind because of his hate. He could easily be reborn as that kind of animal in his next life. And, since the animal imprints the abusive human in its mind, if it goes on to receive a human body, it is likely to become an abusive person. This is a stern reality of the law of the mind.

Also, if you are forced into a war, you have to face the war with the intention of sweeping away the enemy forces in order to defend your nation and your people, not with the intention of shooting down every enemy soldier. If you were to have the mentality of killing each one, a vendetta between you and the dead ones would begin. Whereas if you have the intention of clearing away the entire enemy, it becomes merely a contest between one group and another.

Among the emperors of the Qing Dynasty, six were enlightened. Emperor Kang Xi ruled without killing anyone. The others, when forced into wars, used this expression of clearing the enemy force.

A general, Paek Kae, became insane, however, because of the guilt he felt for murdering thousands of soldiers who had surrendered to him. Also, Cao Cao, in his last moments, was frightened to death by haunting images of all the people who were wrongfully killed due to his mistakes. He died in horror. As Cao Cao's mind weakened, all the regrets imprinted in his mind arose to terrify him.

We plant merit with our minds, and we commit crimes with our minds. With our minds, we imprint images. This one mind is like an artist. It can draw anything, and what it draws is realized. If you surrender your impressions, ideas, thoughts, and so on at the moment they arise without imprinting them on your mind, your mind will not be tainted, just as the lotus flower is not tainted by the muddy water whence it grows.

In Lord Buddha's time, two monks were meditating diligently in a cave on the mountain. One day, the sister of one of the monks brought their daily supplies to the cave, but her brother was not there. Only his friend remained. Out of some strange karmic connection, she and her brother's friend made love. As a result, the monk had to face the tragedy of being banished from the order.

The girl's brother later came back to the cave and heard the story from his sad and distressed friend, a spiritual seeker who had committed an irreversible sin and whose hope of enlightenment was over. He could only agonize in deep despair. After the other monk heard the story, he accused his own sister of crushing his friend's eternity. He put all the blame upon her for his friend's banishment, and he killed her.

Enlightenment, which he felt was more important than his sister's life, might just have been in his eyes a sole wish, or a bitter grudge, that all spiritual seekers carry. Perhaps they consider enlightenment more important than life itself, and their struggle to become enlightened for many lifetimes is almost a vengeance.

One, banished, and the other, a murderer, together they went to see Venerable Upali. Clinging to a last strand of hope, they told him what had happened and asked Venerable Upali if people like them could still be saved. Venerable Upali bluntly said that salvation was impossible for them even if they were to repent.

The two monks lost all hope and began lamenting. Just then,

Vimalakirti, who was passing by, saw them with his wisdom-eye. He realized that their good roots had in fact been planted deeper than those of Venerable Upali. He had to save their dead minds, so he began a Dharma lecture to the three of them.

Venerable Upali, you should not make their sins any heavier. You have to end their worries and remorse so that their minds will not shake any more. The true nature of sin is neither within, without, nor in between. As the Lord Buddha has said, "If the mind is impure, the sentient being is impure, and if the mind is pure, the sentient being is pure." Mind is neither within, without, nor in between. And since the mind is this way, so is the sin. Likewise, everything else is the same way: nothing can exist beyond its true nature. Venerable Upali, when the mind has attained enlightenment, does the mind have any defilement? No, it does not. Likewise, delusions are pure if there is no impurity. If there is no wrong thought, the mind is pure. Being attached to the self is defilement, and not being attached to the self is purity. Like the haze, the moon's reflection on water, and an image reflected in a mirror, all conditioned things are created by delusion. Only the one who knows this is enlightened.

At that moment, a bright ray of hope shone into their dark and hopeless hearts, and the two monks were able to awaken the pure *bodhi* mind once more.

SCOLDING TAINTS THE MIND

Long ago, many bandits roamed the mountains, and they often captured monks. It was said that, less than three years after their capture, the monks began to commit the same crimes, crimes to which they once had been vehemently opposed.

During those three years, every time the captured monks called the bandits "cruel robbers" and "horrible murderers" and watched their acts in horror, the monks photographed those images in their minds. Eventually, those images became their minds. It is very hard to control a mind that has become hardened due to imprinting images of harsh scolding based on conscience and morality.

There are many such examples of people becoming what they criticize, after scolding other people's actions with their minds: the child who became a stutterer after teasing another stuttering child, the daughter-in-law who criticized her mother-in-law and became worse than her mother-in-law, and so on. They all learn while they scold. Every time you see someone else's fault, you should know that such criticizing is your own mind and be able to surrender that mind.

The mind is like a film. If you develop what you have photographed in your mind, it becomes your life. What you imprint on your mind gets played like a movie on a screen called the universe. You yourself become a true actor. When, however, you surrender all the images in your mind, your weary journey also ends.

Two

Surrendering the Mind
to Buddha

JOY AT SEEING YOUR KARMIC HINDRANCES

Once, a certain *bosallim*, or female Buddhist practitioner, went to the New Year's Day prayer gathering at the Temple of the Seven Buddhas. Despite the cold weather, many practitioners were prostrating themselves or reciting Buddha's name all night in front of a stone Buddha that stood in the middle of the temple grounds.

Since the bosallim was wearing many layers of clothing, she felt uncomfortable in her wool coat. She took off her coat and hung it in a room, then bowed and prayed in front of the stone Buddha until dawn. By that time it had gotten colder, so she went back to the room to get her coat so that she might continue praying.

The room had been heated all night by a large fire, and it was so hot that some of the floor mats were slightly burnt. A couple of bosallims were sleeping on the floor instead of praying all night. The scene did not please her. She looked everywhere for her coat and finally found someone sleeping on top of it so as to lessen the heat from the floor. Filled with rage, she examined the coat and found that it was all wrinkled, with some spots even slightly burnt.

She was about to wake the woman who was sleeping on top of the coat and yell at her, but she restrained herself, thinking, "Since the coat is already in this condition, yelling at her will not iron out the wrinkles or repair the burns." She also rationalized that, on her way up to the temple, she could have ripped the coat by getting it stuck on a branch, or lost it entirely, so she convinced herself it was a good thing that only this much damage had occurred.

After her trip, the bosallim came to me and asked me if showing such restraint is how the practice of surrendering is done. Surrendering, however, does not mean restraining or rationalizing one's emotion like that. The moment she thought it was not proper for those women to sleep on the floor, the scolding mind of anger had already surfaced in her mind. The person who practices surrendering well without losing mindfulness would have started to surrender his or her criticism at that very moment. If she had surrendered well at that moment, she probably would not have been so angry when she first found someone sleeping on her coat. If she were not able to do that, she could have at least surrendered her anger the moment she was overwhelmed with rage, even though it was a little late. Instead, she let her anger escape. Surrendering does not mean going through a process of restraining or rationalizing one's emotion, but rather surrendering that emotion directly by reciting Buddha Maitreya's name, *Mireukjon Yeoraebul.*

The instant anger arises in you, you should cleanse it from your mind and be free of it immediately. You should surrender your anger until there is no remnant of it left in you. Also, you should practice surrendering in such a way that the time it takes to cleanse the discriminative notion from your mind gradually diminishes.

Hardened karmic hindrances accumulated in your mind can be surrendered only if they are first revealed through external shocks, just as we remove the dirt in the bottom of a well by stirring its water with a long stick and collecting the surfacing sediments. There is a saying that goes, "Liberation is being happy to see your karmic hindrances arise." This shows us the attitude of a spiritual seeker: always ready.

NOT HOLDING ON TO DELUSIONS

Once I had to visit a senior acquaintance of mine, so I bought some strawberries at the marketplace before I went over to his home. An elderly lady of the household washed the strawberries with just a little water from a small kettle and put them out in a bowl to serve to the guests. I thought the strawberries should have been washed many times with more water to clean off the dirt, bugs, and pesticides. When I saw her washing them with only one bowl of water, I did not think the berries would be clean enough.

Because I am very particular about cleanliness, Master Baek once called me a person "who would even wash water before drinking it." There was no way I would eat those strawberries.

How uncomfortable it is to have the notion of uncleanliness in one's mind! Even though I did not touch the strawberries, I imprinted dirty strawberries in my mind, which will cause me later to pick and eat only dirty fruit. And if I had eaten those strawberries, my uncomfortable feeling would probably have continued, and I might have had to vomit. Or, since I would have felt that bacteria were running around in my stomach, I might have had to go to a hospital right away to feel better.

All these notions are one mind's working. Whether one actually eats the strawberries or not, surrendering a single notion of uncleanliness without keeping it in one's mind, until that notion disappears from one's mind, is the true practice of surrendering.

If you surrender the notion of uncleanliness, you could

either eat or not eat the strawberries depending on the situation, but there is no discomfort from your "notion of uncleanliness." Thus, you would remain calm. A calm and indifferent mind is evidence that you have surrendered the discriminating mind.

SURRENDERING WHILE
WATCHING THE MIND

The practice of constantly watching one's mind is the basis of spiritual practice. If you did not look to other people or objects but always looked into your mind, your mind would not leave you to follow the people you meet on the streets. When your mind is always with the reverence of surrendering, you are being mindful.

Since you do not know when basic karmic hindrances such as laziness, hatred, or lust will arise from your inner world, absentmindedness should be avoided as much as walking on thin ice. Being absentminded means you are not watching your mind carefully.

Timing is very important in the practice of surrendering. A violent karmic hindrance is especially difficult to surrender after it has already surfaced. While constantly watching your mind, you should start surrendering the moment a hindrance tries to take its position and surface in your mind. By the time it plants its roots and spreads its branches, it is very hard to surrender.

Once, a bosallim had an automobile accident. After the accident, she became frightened of cars at the mere sight of one. When she had to walk in the streets, she was in constant fear, and if she had to ride in a car, she would hide her face behind newspapers. This continued even six months after the accident.

I recommended that she read the Diamond Sutra and also

intensely surrender her fears and the memory of the accident whenever they arose in her mind. I asked her to surrender with strong determination, so as not to lose her mindfulness even for a moment—especially if she had to ride in a car. After she had tried it for fifteen days, she became totally liberated from the fears that she had imprinted in her mind, and seeing cars did not bother her anymore.

The bosallim freed herself in fifteen days from fears that she had imprinted in her storehouse consciousness for six months. If she had been proficient in surrendering daily at the time of the accident, she would have been able to surrender her rising fearful intuition the moment the accident occurred, or right before it happened. If she had been able to completely surrender at that moment, in that split second, she might have been able to free herself from the karmic causes that resulted in the accident, thus avoiding the accident altogether. Even if that were not the case, her karmic retribution would have diminished, and she could have lessened the damage of the accident. Also, since her fears would have decreased in accord with her surrendering, she would have experienced less mental trauma. Even after the accident, if she had surrendered her shock as soon as possible, her suffering would not have lasted for six months.

It may safely be said that we are devoting ourselves to spiritual practice in order to use it just once—at the critical moment of our death. Therefore, in order not to forget your practice at shocking moments, you should always practice watching your mind without losing mindfulness.

The Buddha once asked one of his students, "What is the span of human life?"

The student answered, "It is a couple of days, Lord."

The Buddha said, "You do not know the practice yet."

The Buddha asked another student, "What is the span of human life?"

The student answered, "It is the time between meals, Lord."

The Buddha replied, "You also do not know the practice yet."

Again, he asked a different student, "What is the span of human life?"

The student answered, "It is the time between inhaling and exhaling, Lord."

The Buddha said, "You indeed know the practice."

Spiritual practice lies in not losing our mindfulness even in such a short moment as the time between breaths. Thus we should practice surrendering moment after moment.

If you hold on to the endless thoughts and inner discriminations arising in your mind, they will cause illness. If you suppress them, they will explode. But if you surrender those delusions to Buddha, then the mind that has been emptied will be completely filled with Buddha's radiance.

Swiftly surrender arising discriminative notions to Buddha

If there were all sorts of sediments—such as pieces of paper, rice, leaves—in the bottom of a large, deep well, what would you do to clean it? If the well had too much water and if the water kept flowing in, so that you could not pump out the water from the well, you would have to stir the water with a paddle. As the water swirled, all the sediments would rise to the surface. Then, you could clean the well by simply sitting on the side and collecting the surfacing waste with a bowl.

Our minds are like the well. There are many karmic hindrances that have settled in the bottom of our minds here and there. If we were mindful in our everyday lives and immediately surrendered to Buddha the karmic hindrances rising from the bottom of our minds, our minds would be cleansed. The paddle that stirs the well is like the shocks from outside that stir our minds. The waste that rises is like our karmic hindrances that we have to surrender, and collecting the dirt with a bowl is like the practice of surrendering.

When you continue to surrender, you surrender the notion of

"everyday life," the notion of "not losing the mindfulness," the notion of "discriminating minds," and you even surrender the notion of "surrendering to Buddha." Furthermore, even the afterthoughts of those thoughts are surrendered.

All arising inner discriminations are only my mind

When we are scolded by someone, anger erupts in our minds, and we decide the one who scolded us is a terrible person. But if the same person praises us, joy—that has been dwelling in our minds—arises to praise him or her as a nice person.

Whether I think the other person is nice or terrible, it is only an opinion in my mind, and this opinion has nothing to do with the other person. Instead of looking into our own minds, we usually project our discriminating minds on to others and quarrel with them. If there is no hatred in me, I will not hate others, and if there is no anger in me, I will not be angry with others. If the hatred in my mind is extreme, a person who bothers me will be hated to the extent that there is hatred in me.

Like ice melts away under the sun, karmic hindrances melt away under the radiance of the Buddha

When anger arises, intensely surrender it by reciting *Mireukjon Yeoraebul* to that emotion. Your karmic hindrance will melt away little by little each time you recite Buddha's name, just as ice melts away in the sunshine.

Anger arises because of external disturbances, and soon it subsides back into your mind again. If you intensely surrender the anger before it settles back, it will melt away just as much as you have surrendered.

Even if you were able to surrender your anger only so much, the rage that seemed to suffocate you would disappear, and it would bother you only a little. If you surrender it over and over, so that there is no anger left in you, then even if you were humiliated by others, you would simply be calm since there would be no anger in you. You might even be able to give them a peaceful smile.

This is an enlightened person's level. Whether it is the angry mind, sad mind, despising mind, or greedy mind, if you surrender it, you can be freed from it. With *Mireukjon Yeoraebul*'s white radiance, there is no karmic hindrance from which we cannot free ourselves. Even if one of your karmic hindrances were as thick as the earth itself, if you did not miss your chance to intensely surrender it, it could be melted away.

Making offerings with one's mind is what makes Buddha happy

Some people say that presenting nice flowers or fruits to Buddha is the true offering. They argue that surrendering karmic hindrances—such as our suffering minds or hatred—to Buddha cannot be considered a true offering. The reason Buddha came to this world, however, was to enlighten all sentient beings. Therefore, offering up one's discriminations, thereby getting closer and closer to enlightenment, is the service that will make him the happiest. The merit of making a saint happy is the merit that lights up the entire universe.

When you surrender your repulsive karmic hindrances, one by

one, 84,000 discriminative notions become one less: 83,999. If you are freed from one discrimination, one bright light takes the vacated place in your mind; if you surrender two discriminative notions, two lights will take their place. Eventually, when you surrender all 84,000 discriminating minds, bright light fills up all the emptied places in your mind and lights up the entire universe.

When your mind is deeply tranquil, when the brightness of your mind is complete within and without, your mind will know all things without a shred of doubt. This brightness or radiance can mean the nondual wisdom that perceives the true nature of things, rather than actual light or luminosity. That state of powerful energy and joyous white radiance is a state that defies human description. Only with reverence may we serve Buddha well—*barwon*, I offer this won!

ANALOGY FROM THE AVALOKITESHVARA SUTRA

Tang Dynasty's Han Yu once went to see Zen Master Tai Dian and asked him, "According to the Avalokiteshvara Sutra, if a storm and tidal waves are about to overturn a ship and send everyone on it to a land of demons, and even one person among the panic-stricken crowd were to recite *Namu Gwanse-eum Bosal* (Bodhisattva Avalokiteshvara), the water would be calmed and the disaster avoided. Why is that?"

Zen Master Tai Dian answered, "I heard some bitch got laid and bore a son of a bitch. Was that your mother?"

To a powerful man of the Tang Dynasty, this was an outrageous insult. Han Yu wanted to pull out his sword and strike down the master at once, but since he had been embarrassed by the master before, he suppressed his humiliation instead and left the place. He later told the story to a student of Master Tai Dian, and the student said, "How much better could the master have lectured you on that? That was an excellent lesson."

Dumbfounded, Han Yu questioned him further. The monk went on, "In sutras, there are many analogies to cultivating one's mind. The Avalokiteshvara Sutra is the same way. The heart of that analogy is to purify the anger, which destroys one's surroundings, from the mind by reciting Avalokiteshvara Bodhisattva's name. When you hurt others and quarrel with others because of your anger, it is like being in the same danger as the boat with many people that is about to be shipwrecked in a storm.

When you surrender the anger by reciting Avalokiteshvara's name, your mind will become peaceful, as if the storm and tidal waves had stopped, and your surroundings will also be at peace. Because the master is full of compassion, he gave you an excellent lecture. He wanted you to actually experience his answer, despite the anger it would evoke in you."

After listening to the monk's explanation, Han Yu said to him, "Your explanation has awakened me even more than the master's sermon," and he thanked the monk.

Since the old days, it has been said that "anger is the fire in one's mind that burns away all of one's virtuous deeds." Anger should be absolutely surrendered by reciting Buddha's name.

The greedy mind must also be surrendered every time it arises, in order to awaken to one's true needs. Also, because one cannot easily realize one's own ignorant or arrogant mind, it should be surrendered the moment one notices it. Think of the other person as Shakyamuni Buddha's incarnation, who has come to teach you. And while acknowledging that you are the lowest person in the world, generate the mind of trying to learn from others.

THREE POISONS: GREED, HATRED, AND ARROGANCE

Greed

Because a human being has a body, he needs a house to live in, food to eat, and clothes to wear. However, even if our physical needs are taken care of, we still crave with our mind. This craving mind is called *tamsim*.

If you try to eradicate greed from your mind, you will feel impoverished. Therefore, you should realize what you truly need and take care of these needs. You should also realize the amount of merit that has been previously planted in your mind.

There are two types of greed: the craving that wants to possess material goods, called *gantamsim*, and the craving that wants to possess a person, which we see in relationships between men and women, called—*eumtamsim*.

When you cling to things—whether physical or spiritual—you condition yourself to have a long body, like that of a snake, in your next life. Because you are trying to grasp much with a small body, your body will become longer. Before you cling to things such as a higher position, before you crave it, invoke a won to Buddha, wishing that everyone else would ascend to a higher position.

Even enlightenment becomes problematic if you cling to it. If you devote yourself to the spiritual practice in order to serve Buddha, you will be enlightened. But if you say, "I am going to get enlightened," then enlightenment becomes very difficult. Such an intention is greed, therefore, you should surrender that greed—that ardent desire to become enlightened—to Buddha and learn to truly follow the path of enlightenment.

Greed is an unhealthy mind and the source of misfortune. It should be purified both by realizing one's true needs and by practicing charity toward others without expecting any reward. Look at the mind of one who has not eaten for a day, or the mind of one who has lost his or her loved one to someone else. Such a desperate mind is the mind of a wild beast. Such wild emotions should be surrendered intensely to Buddha in order to liberate them from your mind.

After getting rid of your greed, confronting others' greed is like putting a cow made of clay into water. Once you get rid of the karmic hindrance in your own mind, others' karmic hindrances will melt away too.

Anger (Hatred)

Just as ashes are the only remains of fire, destruction is the only remnant of the path of anger. Anger brings poison to the mind and fiery karmic retribution to the body. An angry mind is an unhealthy mind. It is a source of misfortune and disaster. An angry mind is like a fire—it dries our blood and burns our flesh. Whether it is heart-stricken vengeance, intense hatred, or fright and anxiety, there is no discriminating mind that cannot be purified by the white radiance of *Mireukjon Yeoraebul.* When an ironlike, suffocating, karmic hindrance arises in you, if you surrender that to Buddha, it pleasantly melts away like ice melting under the sun, and your mind calms down, attaining wisdom.

At first it might take thirty minutes or an hour to surrender your anger. Later, it could be shortened to just five minutes or even one minute. After a while, you will be able to surrender your anger by reciting *Mireukjon Yeoraebul* just once. Sometimes, right before the anger arises, the very moment it begins to form in you, you might be able to surrender your anger just by calling out the first character, "*Mi.*"

Always look into your mind. The reaction that arises from others' praise is your mind, and the reaction that arises from others' scolding is also your mind. Therefore, do not look outside of your mind, but look inside it and completely surrender the arising thoughts and emotions. After getting rid of your anger, confronting others' anger is, once again, like putting a cow made of clay into water.

Arrogance

If you desire to be treated well and to be served by others, you are only practicing attachment to your body. If you are not willing to learn from the world, your wisdom cannot grow. You will be separated from the wisdom of the universe, and yours will be a life of complete darkness.

If you practice the arrogant mind, you start to dislike everyone. An arrogant mind is an unhealthy mind, and it is a source of disaster, misfortune, and no wisdom. It presents darkness to the mind and sufferings to the body. An arrogant person treats himself like his own enemy.

Instead, see everyone as a Buddha. You will discover many of Buddha's actions from these numerous future Buddhas, and you will be able to learn from them. Thus, through these Buddhas' scoldings and punishments, it will be hard not to examine yourself and hard not to be awakened by them.

King Yu of China bowed to anyone who pointed out his faults. He thanked them very deeply, because without their insight he would have had to live with the heavy burden of his limitations.

One of Confucius's students said to Confucius, "Look over there: a thief is being taken away by a policeman." Confucius then said, "I guess your teacher is passing by." The student then asked Confucius, "Why is he my teacher?" Confucius replied, "Isn't that thief ruining his life to teach you and everyone else a great lesson—to show us the results of crime? When we know that the events of the world are our lessons and teachers, we further our drive for learning. Our realizations will illuminate our wisdom."

If you think your practice has progressed much, remember that such belief comes only from your mind—it is neither the result of invoking a won to Buddha nor of not invoking a won. Surrender your belief that your practice has progressed much, as well as the belief that your practice has not progressed much. If you cling to the notion that you have been practicing for a long time, you have only that notion in your mind, and there is no place for Buddha. Therefore, awaken your conviction again and again. Renew your determination, over and over, and surrender even the notion that you have surrendered.

MIND'S POISON AND BODY'S DISEASE

In many cases, the actions of our minds control our diseases. If a cow drinks water it becomes milk, but if a snake drinks water it becomes poison. Depending on how we use our minds, the results of our diseases are infinitely varied.

The poison generated by one's mind comes out mostly in the form of greed or anger. If the poison spreads through greed, it causes diseases, such as stomach cancer, ulcer, or gastritis, in one's digestive organs. If the poison spreads through anger, it causes diseases in one's respiratory organs, such as the lungs or bronchial tubes.

Swelling in your head or swelling that sprouts on the back of your neck, on your thigh, or on your legs is caused by the poison generated in your mind spreading to your body. Even fatigue can be seen as being caused by the poison in your mind together with your body's exhaustion. If you spew out the mind's poison through your mouth, it becomes negative karma of the mouth. Someone who accumulated much negative karma of the mouth in his past life, or who spewed out many poisonous words, has faulty teeth.

Sometimes the mind's poison can spread directly to the environment. Just as in the Korean saying, "A woman's slander can bring frost in May and June," one person's poisonous mind can torment the people around him. If a manager of a company has a bad day at home and vents his anger on his section chief, the section chief would then vent his anger on his foreman, and the foreman would vent his anger on hundreds of factory workers.

The poison would then spread like the ripples formed by a rock thrown into a pond. Thus, the health of the mind is directly related to the health of the body and to the health of society.

May we thoroughly surrender the three poisons, so that we can serve Buddha well, barwon!

SIX PERFECTIONS

Charity *(bosi)*. Treat others with the mind of giving, and practice doing works that have no reward. The perfection of *bosi* purifies the mind of greed.

Ethical restraint *(jigye)*. Do not dwell on regrets. Try to lessen the regrettable incidents in your life. The perfection of *jigye* purifies the mind of anger.

Patient endurance *(inyok)*. See everyone as a Buddha. It is for you to realize and learn the Buddha's perfection of *inyok*. The perfection of *inyok* purifies the mind of ignorance and arrogance.

Zealous effort *(jeongjin)*. The first three perfections are the laws that you should apply to the world as a human being. If they are right, then practice them with diligence. This is the perfection of *jeongjin*.

Stability of mind *(seonjeong)*. Through the practices above, as time passes, your mind will become calm. This is the perfection of *seonjeong*.

Wisdom *(banya)*. When you are used to these perfections, your mind will become peaceful and attain wisdom. Thus, you will have no doubts in your actions. This is the perfection of *banya*.

— *from a Dharma lecture by Master Baek*

T h r e e

Purifying the Mind
Enlightening the Mind

SURRENDERING THE HATRED

One human being hating another is a great tragedy. But, since we are human, we live with hatred in our minds. Buddha called this hatred suffering. The exchange of hatred between family members or between colleagues at work, for example, is the suffering of having to live with someone you consider your enemy.

However, one who serves Buddha surrenders his or her hatred to Buddha instead of blaming others. When you dislike someone, do not look to that person for the reasons behind your hatred, but rather surrender the hatred rising within you. If you have difficulty finding and focusing on the rising hatred within you, surrender it by reciting *Mireukjon Yeoraebul* to the face of the one you hate or to his or her name.

Otherwise, invoke a won to Buddha for the person you hate. Until the hatred in you disappears, invoke such wons as: "May _____ awaken faith and reverence within himself, so that he can plant great merit before Buddha, barwon, I offer this won."

Since the mind wishing the hated person to accumulate great merit is your own mind, you will accumulate the merit before the other person does. Accumulating merit makes you more generous and gentle, and your mind does not become too sharp or bitter.

There was a man who detested his coworker. The presence of this coworker was like a thorn in his eye. And because the hatred was mutual, the man suffered unspeakably while working with that person. He once came to visit Master Baek and told him his problem, and Master Baek instructed him to invoke a won for his coworker. So, according to Master Baek's teaching, he invoked this won to Buddha: "May_____awaken faith and devotion to Buddha, so that he can serve Buddha well, barwon."

Because the pain of his hatred was unbearable, he had to carry out the practice many times a day. Sometimes he invoked that won to Buddha over a hundred times a day.

After trying this for a year, he finally cleansed his mind of the hatred. His coworker no longer offended him so much, and he was at peace. Also, since he had opened his heart to Buddha every time he invoked the won, he was full of joy.

The other person, however, was still experiencing the suffering of hell from his own hatred because he did not know how to cultivate his mind. Instead, to let out his repressed hatred, he quietly began criticizing the student of Master Baek who had cultivated his mind. If a third person were to see these two, the one who had cultivated his mind would appear virtuous, while the one who had not cultivated his mind would seem to be a narrow-minded person who only saw others' faults.

He who serves Buddha cultivates his mind by always watching his mind. He does not quarrel with any right or wrong outside of his mind.

HOLY TEACHER TULLE

An old man named Tulle was often hired to work at Sosa Monastery. He gave us a hard time by taking advantage of our lack of knowledge in farming (for we were from Seoul) and of the fact that he had been living in that area longer than we. He tricked us in many ways and worked carelessly while still receiving his full salary.

As a spiritual seeker who had devoted my life to Buddha, I felt I could not forgive his dishonest attitude. I was in charge of the kitchen back then. At the immature age of twenty-six, I could not bear the discomfort of serving such precious food to such a despicable person. Also, because he treated us—those who were training for the path of enlightenment—as laborers like himself and tried to act as our superior, his arrogance seemed ridiculous to me. He was like a thorn in my eye.

Since I could not stand him whenever I saw him, I was forced to intensely surrender my painful hatred by reciting *Mireukjon Yeoraebul*. For fifteen days, I surrendered all hatred that rose within me without letting any of it escape. One day, out of nowhere, I heard a voice saying, "Holy teacher Tulle, holy teacher Tulle." The voice was rich and majestic.

Tulle, the one who caused me to surrender my wicked hatred, was truly a holy teacher to me. I felt thankful to him again and again, for without him, I probably could not have purified this hateful mind of mine.

It is people like him who are my Buddhas. All people who awaken me or make me cultivate my mind are my Buddhas.

Where else would you look for Buddhas? If a person truly realizes that everyone is a Buddha, such a person is probably also a Buddha at peace in that moment.

PURIFYING THE MIND, ENLIGHTENING THE MIND

I entered Sosa monastery at the age of twenty-six and devoted myself to practice for seven years and six months. I had my progress checked every one hundred days. Below are a few episodes that come to mind from these interviews.

About two hundred days into the practice, a large number of parasitic worms came out of my body. The worms had formed each time my thoughts wandered. I had never taken anti-parasitic drugs before, but now as my mind turned towards the bright radiance of Buddha, the parasites could bear it no longer and came out. After this, my complexion was full of warmth.

After four hundred days of studying, a dark reddish toxin resembling a clot of bloody pus was discharged with the feces. The skin around the area felt extremely hot and stung with pain. Our body generates poison whenever we become angry, and causes infections and impurities to accumulate densely in the organs. Often, our anger will be triggered by these impurities, and we become even angrier. Once this poison and these impurities came out, there was no more anger and my mind was at ease. Joyful energy arose from my lower abdomen, and I was so grateful that it brought tears to my eyes.

This quiet strength that I felt in my lower abdomen spread to the rest of the body, like water that flows continuously from a spring, filling the surrounding area with warmth. The pain and anguish that I had felt recently in my mind and body had all disappeared, and it felt like the beginning of a new world. The energy emanating from the *danjeon* (one inch below the navel) brought happiness and warmth to the mind, together with peace and radiance. I was so profoundly moved at being awakened to the newfound bliss of Buddha's realm that I even wondered how such joy could exist in the world. A warm breeze blew in my desolate mind. For the first time, I had glimpsed the brightness of the heavenly realm—perceived by those free from greed, anger and ignorance. I realized that this blissful energy was not mine alone, but that it imbued its whole surroundings with warmth. I was astonished at how different the world seemed, and realized that the world itself is inherently at peace. It appears busy, noisy and painful simply because of our discriminations.

THE PERSON WHO ENLIGHTENS ME
IS MY BUDDHA

There was a monk who used to hate cleaning and kitchen duties, but after the abbot of his monastery made him do those chores during his one-hundred-day meditation retreat, those tasks became enjoyable to him. This was a result of cleansing his mind of the dislike for work.

How fortunate he is now that he has no aversion to his duties and is full of joy! Because there is that much less distaste in his mind, his body has become much more cheerful. For that monk, the abbot of the monastery who forced him to do the work and made him cultivate his mind by doing so is his Buddha.

People who enlighten me are all my Buddhas. Instead of trying to find Buddhas in high and precious places, shouldn't you be able to find your Buddhas in your town, in your marketplaces, and in your streets? Everyone has valuable and enlightening qualities. If you learned and practiced those qualities, it would be like meeting the Buddha and practicing his teachings. There are plenty of Buddhas around us all the time: Buddhas in our homes, Buddhas at our workplaces, Buddhas in our streets, Buddhas in our buses...

SURRENDERING THE ATTACHMENT TO THE BODY

In the process of cleansing my basic karmic hindrances, I was scolded and often hit by my teacher. It wounded my pride as a senior practitioner, especially when he scolded me harshly in front of the other practitioners. I did not know how to deal with the embarrassment and the humiliation. The sorrow and discontent rising sharply within me only caused more pain.

At those times, if I kept staring at my painful mind and surrendered it by reciting *Mireukjon Yeoraebul*, the one who was getting scolded did not feel like me, but someone else. Eventually, I stopped becoming embarrassed and hurt by my teacher's scolding. Such equanimity was evidence that my sharply arising ego was melting away through the practice of surrendering.

Even on hot summer days, when my mind could not tolerate the heat, I surrendered my discomfort and it lessened the pain. The heat then became bearable. It may have been a little hot outside, but I no longer had to put up with my suffocating annoyance.

One time I was sitting in the ditches of a bean field, pulling up weeds the day after it had rained. It felt as if the heat would suffocate me—not the slightest breeze blew along the ditch. On top of that, the heat rose up from the ground, and the sun's rays struck on my back. It was one o'clock in the afternoon, the hottest time of the day.

At that moment, while I intensely surrendered the notion

that the heat was unbearable, sweat began to drip from my head down my back, running down the trough of my spine like cool refreshing raindrops on my skin. If the heat of anger is in your mind, you cannot bear any additional heat from outside. But, since I was surrendering the stuffy heat in my mind as soon as it came up, the heat was not accumulating in me. Therefore, I did not feel as much pain.

During the seven and a half years of my life at Sosa, between 12:00 P.M. and 3:00 P.M. of every hot summer day, I overcame the heat—while carrying a heavy rack on my back, while cutting grass, while pulling weeds, while tilling the soil, and while pulling carts. I did not give in to my mind when it complained about the heat. Even during the middle of the day, my working mentality was one of continual surrendering—even when my sweaty clothes stuck to my body, leaving me sticky and disgusting, the practice of surrendering continued. It was a practice that dealt fiercely with my ego.

Once I milked a cow while taking in its steamy body heat with my whole body—my upper body pressed against the cow's leg and my forehead pressed against her stomach. It was unbearable at that moment. After doing the same with three more cows, I had no strength left in my hands and arms. My shirt was full of sweat, as if it had been soaked in water. On top of that, when the cow used its manure-caked tail to chase away the flies and whipped my face and eyes instead, it quickly stirred up my disgust and my ego. Those tense moments—my face covered with cow manure and sweat pouring out of me like raindrops, milking a cow with a bucket between my knees to protect it from being kicked over—those were important moments in the cultivation of my mind.

This practice of surrendering while working, constantly surrendering more and more, is itself the very reverence that speaks "Lord Buddha." In this reverence, there is not even an "I" who generates reverence. The worst conditions then become ideal conditions for cultivating one's mind.

Once, I put too much cow dung on my rack, and I could barely get up and keep my balance because my legs were so shaky. I had to carry the rack of dung over a hill with an incline of almost twenty degrees to a field about two-thirds of a mile away from the monastery. Since I was used to taking the rack there without stopping, I tried to surrender the feeling of discomfort from the heavy load and to arrive without stopping. Meanwhile, my body was crying out in pain. Step by step, with all my strength, I surrendered the burden of that heavy load while fiercely asking myself, "What is the true nature of this thing that's complaining about the heavy load?" It was a matter of life and death. Not once did I give in to myself. Because I was consistently able to surrender the attachment to my body, my mind was like a never-losing battlefield.

Sometimes, as I carried crops from the distant fields or walked down the dark mountain path by myself at night, it felt as if someone were pulling me from behind. When my whole body became overwhelmed by the dark energy from behind, I looked straight ahead and surrendered the horrible feeling of wanting to look back. If too much fear arose in my mind, I knelt and surrendered it on the spot by reciting *Mireukjon Yeoraebul* for at least thirty minutes. I then descended the mountain with a peaceful mind. In the winter, I surrendered while kneeling on top of the ice-covered path in the mountains.

I held out with the attitude of "Here, take this body if you want!" and surrendered my fear. When I came down from the mountain after surrendering my fear, I felt extremely happy.

When I used to think of my mother, who became a widow at twenty-three, my heart felt as if it were being torn apart. Besides, my one sister had gone to Germany, leaving my mother alone in our hometown. This was a strong attachment, a blood tie, and being able to surrender the karmic attachment of blood ties is very important for spiritual seekers. Sexual desire can be surrendered relatively easily without losing mindfulness, because such desire can be embarrassing, but karmic ties to a parent, especially to a widowed mother, are hard indeed to surrender. When I was finally freed from that karmic attachment, the world became simply refreshing, tranquil, and bright. My doubts were resolved and insightful wisdom arose.

There is power that comes from overcoming attachment to one's body. This power leads to eradicating doubts and knowing the true nature of things. Realizations come naturally through the practice of surrendering.

PURIFY ANGER TO ACHIEVE BUDDHAHOOD

There is a saying, "Purify yourself of anger to achieve Buddhahood." Anger should be completely cleansed from the mind. However, surrendering anger is as painful as tearing out one's heart.

I had so much trouble surrendering my anger at Sosa. Every time anger from my past lives surfaced, it was hell beyond comparison. For an entire day, my mind would be upset, my inner body would burn, and I was full of complaints. Since my mind was burning, my face also burned darkly. Whatever I did, my mind was not at ease, and it was constantly bubbling up. Even the sound of the wind, the sound of a door being slammed, or even someone smiling, angered me.

For people who do not have much anger in them, this is probably hard to understand. Even though they live on the same land and in the same environment, heavenly beings and hellish beings are divided according to the state of their minds. One group lives in happiness, and the other lives in constant complaint, hatred, and spite.

One time I surrendered an angry mind as if my life depended on it. The anger surfaced in me while I was working in the field, and I sat down on the spot, focused my vision, and stopped my breathing. I was worried that, if I remained standing, the feeling of too much wind on my legs, body, and head would destroy my concentration, or that my vision might be too wide and distract me from my surrendering. So I sat and looked down. Also, since the sound of my breathing might break my concentration, I concentrated my mind and body on a single extended breath and fiercely surrendered the anger in me by reciting *Mireukjon Yeoraebul*. Since the sound of reciting might distract my surrendering, I recited silently. By surrendering with such strong determination, I was able to take care of the anger with two or three long breaths. In one breath, I focused on reciting *Mireukjon Yeoraebul* more than ten times, as if I were focusing sunlight through a convex lens to burn a piece of paper.

When you practice your surrendering like this, the root of the anger gets cleansed, and your heart feels very refreshed. Because anger is an emotion to which you have been conditioned, if you surrender it to Buddha's radiance every time it arises, you can liberate yourself from it. Furthermore, as you sense the Buddha's realm of light, your wisdom-eye will open and you will perceive the true nature of things. Once you overcome the root of your anger, the realm of wisdom will open up for you, and the bright and refreshing Dharma bliss will lead to pure reverence. I am so grateful that there is a Buddha who will accept this suffering from me.

Lord Buddha, Master Baek, if it were not for the method of surrendering that you realized, how could I have ever surrendered that mind of anger? I thank you!

THE BURNING FIRE

Once, when Lord Buddha was passing by a mountain with his students, a fire started on the mountain. The crackling red-hot fire gave off scorching heat.

Buddha then lectured: "Monks, there is a fire that is hotter than that flame on the mountain. It is the fire that burns in your mind called the fire of lust. The fire that burns fiercely on the mountain only burns your body. But the fire of lust—raging in your mind, desiring beautiful women—burns your mind, too." As Buddha let out his lion's roar, some were greatly awakened, some threw up blood, and some ran away.

Buddha also said that if there were one more thing like sexual desire, no one would attain Buddhahood. Overcoming sexual desire was difficult back then, and it is difficult now. Since sexual desire originates within the mind, however, by surrendering that craving mind to Buddha, you can, in the end, be liberated even from that mind.

If you restrain or suppress your sexual desires too much, though, it can cause harmful side effects to the body. And if a spiritual seeker mutilates his body because he cannot handle his sexual desires, it is hard for him to become enlightened due to the regret that he imprints on the mind. What we should do is to surrender arising desires with great reverence.

Scientists have found through research that generating reverence and praying rapidly reduces the hormone that causes sexual desire. In other words, sexual desires arise when we are idle and unmindful. If the mind does not arise, then the body is not aroused. If you intensely recite *Mireukjon Yeoraebul* on the physical part of the body that is aroused, it will calm down as if nothing has happened. Then, afterwards, recite *Mireukjon Yeoraebul* on the mind itself. Sexual desires can be surrendered in this way.

If sexual desire arises very strongly, it may be a result of excessive nutrition, in which case you should decrease the amount of food you eat. Another method of calming your mind and body when sexual desires arise is to touch your ears with both hands. For those who live in a monastery, walking around the Dharma Hall while reciting Buddha's name with hands folded is a method of calming the desire. For others, doing jumping jacks, running in the field, performing labor that requires much physical exertion, or taking a bath in cold water are also useful. If you have too much idle time, it is a good idea to get a hobby. In whatever way, this obstacle must be overcome and cleansed.

CHECK THE DOOR LOCK
AT THE THIRD HOUR

A monastery's front gate and fences help to guard spiritual seekers' minds. The mind that practices the three poisons of greed, anger, and arrogance always directs its attention outside the monastery. Gates and fences, however, present a psychological barrier to such distractions. The notion that one is closed in weakens and blocks the karmic force.

The saying "Check the door lock at the third hour of the night" started in reference to disciplining the mind. Master Baek always barred the door and locked the padlock. Even on hot summer days, he slept with his door closed. He always closed the door whenever he went in or out of the room, and he told us to do the same. He taught us this habit as an aid in cultivating the mind.

In cultivating one's mind, monastic rules work as gates and fences. The rules are not to tie people down but to discipline the karmic hindrance that distracts them from their practice. Following the rules gives rise to stability, and stability gives rise to wisdom. By swiftly surrendering the mind that wants to escape the rules, and also by surrendering the mind that wants to follow the rules, your mind becomes healthy and free before the rules. And from freedom your actions will find order.

When the mind's lock is breached, the seeds of temptation and catastrophe immediately take root. If a tiny pinhole is created, a karmic hindrance the size of a bull breaks in. A split second's absentmindedness brings eternal regret. One should always be on guard.

ABOUT THE PRACTICE TIME

The bright energy of the universe starts to rise at three in the morning and lasts until three in the afternoon. So at 3 A.M. the sky is dark but the energy is bright, and at 3 P.M. the sky is bright but the energy is dark. Since our minds also change with the energy of the universe, our minds are clear in the morning but they become cloudy in the afternoon.

When 9 P.M. approaches, negative energy starts to circulate. That is why offerings to spirits are usually made after 9 P.M., and that is also why monks in the monasteries go to bed around 9 P.M. At around 3 A.M. the negative energy begins to disappear, and between 3 A.M. and 5 A.M., the energy is very bright and clear. The Bodhisattva Manjushri is said to hold his Dharma lectures during these hours. When you get up at this hour to practice, you will receive the energy of the universe in full.

It is said that among the ones who get up early in the morning there is rarely a person who is not bright, and among the ones who roam around late at night there is rarely a person who does not face misfortune. By following the energy of the universe— working when there is bright energy and sleeping when the energy is dark—our minds and bodies will become healthy.

For those who cultivate the mind, it is better not to lose the mindfulness of reciting *Mireukjon Yeoraebul* before falling asleep. By doing so, practice continues throughout the night until the moment you wake up. On the other hand, if you fall asleep in an absentminded state, you will remain absentminded throughout your sleep, and your mind will not be clear even when you wake up. It is preferable, also, not to take naps during the day, for then you are practicing the dark mind on a bright day.

DISCRIMINATING MINDS OCCUR IN UNITS OF THREE

Among the discriminations in our minds, some occur every three seconds, some every three minutes, some every thirty minutes, three hours, three days, three weeks, three months, or three hundred years. There are even discriminations that occur every three thousand years.

If you miss your chance to surrender a discrimination that occurs every three thousand years, your enlightenment gets delayed for another three thousand years. Losing the chance to purify from one's mind an inner discrimination that occurs only every three hundred years is also a terrible mistake. You should always be mindful lest you lose your chance to surrender to Buddha the precious offerings that arise only once every couple of lifetimes.

The essence and the life of practice is not losing the chance to surrender the discriminations, which arise and sink in units of three. When a thought arises, you have one more thing to cleanse from your mind, for if you do not cleanse that thought now, you will have to do it in your next life.

While I was training at Sosa, every time I was wrestling with a karmic hindrance that had arisen in me, my teacher would admonish me, saying, "If you do not surrender it now, it will be a burden in your next life." In other words, if I surrendered it instead, it would become the job of this life. He was telling us to solve the "one great aim [of becoming enlightened]" in this very life.

SEE YOUR OWN FACE
AND SURRENDER YOUR FAULTS

Buddha's eyes are called the eyes of the blue lotus. It is said that if your mentality is that of forgiving others' flaws as if they were your own flaws and of disclosing your flaws as if they were others' flaws, then your eyes will look like those of Buddha, wherein the middle of the eye seems slightly closed, and the ends seem slightly open. On the other hand, if your mind is full of the desire to find others' faults, your eyes will be as round as jawbreaker candies—just like a cat's eyes when it is trying to find a mouse.

There are many theories about how one's mentality influences one's physical attributes. It is said, for instance, that if a person has a sharp nose line, his mind is like the sharp edge of a sword. Thus, if he intends to strike someone down and fails to do so, his mind will hit himself back, causing him, in many cases, to have bad lungs. A person with a less forgiving mind is said to have a narrow space between his eyebrows. Such a person should use his mind more gently and generously, and practice a forgiving and understanding mind toward others. Moreover, a person with high cheekbones is said to be opinionated; a person with a straight nose bridge is said to have an honest personality; a person who is cross-eyed is said to have a hard time concentrating his or her mind on one thing; someone whose face is very dark is said to be very greedy, and so on.

The facial features come from the skull features, and the

skull features come from the mind's features. In order for your facial features to change, the way you use your mind should change. In the end, people advertise "I live my life this way" with their faces.

By the time we reach age twenty-seven, through regeneration, even our brain cells have changed, and we have completely different bodies than the ones our parents gave us. We have become totally independent of our parents. Therefore our faces after twenty-seven are not our parents' fault. The way we use our minds continues the building of our faces.

F o u r

Be True
to the Present Present

BE TRUE TO THE PRESENT PRESENT

The past has already gone by, the future is not yet here, and as soon as we say, "the present" it has already become our past. We should be true to each passing moment, which we cannot even truly call "the present."

Because elderly people are attached to the past and live in their memories, thinking, "In the good old days things used to be...," they practice the dead mind. Likewise, young people have only grand blueprints for their future and lack the present foundation from which to gradually fulfill their plans. They practice the delusive mind.

He who can surrender the discriminations that are arising this very moment, who can solve the problem right in front of him without avoiding it, is one who can utilize the present in the present. Such a person is indeed an able person. If you are true to your present present, you will naturally be true to your future future, and you will be true to your past past.

If you do not postpone today's job until tomorrow, quarrel over the right or wrong of yesterday's incident, nor worry about tomorrow's job ahead, then the calm and vitality arising in your mind will make your present more meaningful.

Living one hundred years a day is a sign of an ignorant person. Regretting things that happened five years ago and worrying about things that won't happen until five years from now is a foolishness that should be avoided by a household of spiritual seekers. How fulfilling it would be if we were able to live just twenty-four hours a day! It is difficult to live even twenty-four hours a day, but how peaceful and serene our minds would be if we were able to live just twelve hours a day! As the clock endlessly ticks away, how many of us recognize the gravity of our inability to turn back time? This very moment disappears forever.

To the enlightened mind—which arises from eradicating the discrimination of time that stretches for eons—there is only the present, and the present, which lives in the big present [which encompasses the past, present, and future], is the entire universe. This present is freed from even the chronological characteristic of a beginning and an ending. Whether it is the present of three thousand years ago or the present of this moment, the root is the same: the One Mind. Thus the present is the entire body of life itself, and the moment you are awakened to the present, it is simply enlightenment.

The present might even be the Buddha. The truthful mind is the moment in which the Buddha dwells. When Buddha is enshrined in a mind, that mind's speech and actions are reverent—its behavior is dignified and its spirit is always awake.

Therefore, awaken to the present. Becoming enlightened by being true to the present present is the finest tranquility.

MINDING THE STORE

When you are running a store and business is lagging, instead of being troubled by the lack of customers, you should surrender that troubled feeling. As long as you are stuck with a troubled mind, the mental wave it creates will completely fill the store with an annoying energy. Even if a customer wanted to come in and shop, he or she would sense the negative wave, for human minds are this sensitive, and the customer would lose interest and not go in. And if a customer did come in, the negative wave would make him or her leave quickly.

Surrendering feelings of annoyance and worry is the practice that will attract customers. If you do not let your mind wander or worry, you will be bright and awake, and you can dust the store or organize the merchandise. In the moment you are busy working, your mind is diligent and alive. An alive mind's wave generates vibrant energy, and such energy motivates customers to shop at your store. Even if customers do not come right away, with an alive mind, wisdom and calm arise to solve the problem and look for new possibilities.

An alive mind achieves tangible success in life. The human world is established on the consequences of numerous alive minds. Various colors filled with vibrant energy are brightly leading the world of reality. If business is slow in a rice store, isn't it better if the owner picks the dust from the rice and changes the display of his merchandise to attract some attention to the store, rather than doing nothing and letting his thoughts wander? When an atmosphere of diligence is alive in a store, customers come, attracted by that diligence. This is the businessman's mind of practicing being true to the present.

Thinking one's business is slow should also absolutely be avoided. You should avoid even letting those words out of your mouth. When others ask you how business is, it is better for you to tell them that it is going well. Indeed, you yourself should actually have the mentality that your business is going well. In the end, being successful depends on the conditioning of your mind.

NOT LOSING YOUR MINDFULNESS

A couple of days ago, I heard that someone was walking down the stairs drunk, with his hands in his pockets, and fell down the stairs and died from head injuries. As this example shows, absentmindedness should absolutely be avoided. One who tries to be true to the present would be just as alert walking down the stairs as when he was walking up the stairs. Every time you take a step, you should retain the mindfulness of surrendering by reciting *Mireukjon Yeoraebul.* Just in case, you should be prepared to put your hands out. It helps you in cultivating your mind, and it eliminates any danger.

Also, before we go and meet someone, we usually ponder about how we are going to answer if he or she says this or that, and we think about going to certain places with him or her. However, when we actually meet the person, so many times we learn that our pondering was useless, and the situation ends up being totally different from what we had expected.

Every time your mind ponders, imagining what is going to happen, surrender those thoughts. Instead of following such drifting thoughts, if you keep surrendering those thoughts and reach the nondual state, you might become aware of what is actually going to happen in your meeting. Your mind becomes brighter, giving you the appropriate answers to the other person's questions. Also, your mind's power becomes clear and strong enough to help put him or her at ease.

A POSITIVE MENTALITY

When someone asks us a favor, we usually give a clear "yes" or "no" right away without much consideration. Some matters should be handled in such a way, but if we are always this careless, we might suffer a loss or hurt someone's feelings.

When someone makes a request, a generous person first accepts that person's feelings by communicating, "Yes, I want to help you!" A person with a negative mind, however, initially rejects the request as an imposition. A negative person resists other people's feelings, and there are several possible explanations why. It might be because the negative person is arrogant and does not try to learn from others, or because he is close-minded. If he is angry and unstable, he may simply not have enough sense to accept them. In any case, if the necessary conditions are not there, he does not willingly accept the other person's feelings. If a person starts, however, by constantly practicing the positive mentality of saying, "Yes!" then the positive action of saying yes comes naturally.

Whether or not you actually end up carrying out the favor for the other person, he will be satisfied and his mind will be calmed if you first accept his feelings. Since human minds are typically weak, a rejection of his feelings will cause vengeance to surge in his mind. When such a poisonous mind is provoked, isn't it painful for everyone? An accomplished person is able to embrace such a mind, to soothe it, and give it different perspectives.

The accepting mind is the mind that wants to satisfy the

other person. By practicing such a mentality, many possibilities for exchanging virtue between yourself and the other person arise. Because you have accepted the other's feelings by saying, "Yes!", if you then say, "Let's think of the possibilities," the other person will be content. If there is a possibility, the other person's request will be fulfilled. What happens, however, when what the other has asked turns out to be impossible? Since you first said, "Let's think of the possibilities," then, when the other person responds, you can tell him or her, "I am in such and such a situation" and ask, "What do you think I should do?" In this way, you can resolve the situation regardless of the end result, neither of your feelings would be hurt, and the intended goal would be accomplished.

Solving these types of problems with humility is called the housekeeping of one's mind.

THE MIND THAT SHELTERS NO IMPOSSIBILITIES

I once knew a person who ran a rice mill. At his mill, whenever he saw the strong workers easily picking up large sacks of rice, he used to think, "I should be able to do that," and he became envious of them. He knew that there was no way he could lift a sack of rice with his limited strength at that time. So every time he saw a sack of rice, he endlessly surrendered his sense of impossibility by reciting *Mireukjon Yeoraebul.*

One day, one of the sacks of rice appeared very small to him. He lifted it up and threw it, and it landed far away. Everyone around looked at him with shocked expressions. Since he had been surrendering the notions of heaviness, to the extent that he had surrendered those notions, that much Dharma power had been awakened in him. With that Dharma power, he was able to throw the sack of rice.

If you pass on to the next life with a belief in your inability to do a certain thing, then in your next life, you will still not be able to do that thing. Without even talking about the life to come, if you practice the mind of impossibility in this life, even things that are possible now will become impossible. When you surrender the notion of both possibility and impossibility to Buddha, however, and face your problems without any preconceived notions, you will be able to accomplish your goals naturally.

BE FREE FROM PRECONCEIVED NOTIONS

Once a man came to see Master Baek at Sosa and said, "I can't breathe too well, sir." Our teacher told him, "Surrender the mind that believes you can't breathe too well to Buddha, and breathe as much as you want." The man had been suffering from tuberculosis for a long time and his asthma had caused difficulties in breathing, but after he had visited our teacher, his asthma improved. Prior to his visit, he was not able to breathe well simply because of the single notion that he could not breathe well.

Likewise, one whose single notion is loneliness is always lonely. One whose single notion is poverty is always poor. One whose single notion is that of a beggar lives his entire life as a beggar. One whose single notion is arrogance always thinks that he or she is superior to everyone else. Since such a person does not try to learn from either the wise or the world, he or she runs into many failures.

A third grader lives with a third grader's wisdom, knowledge, and use of the mind. If he believes his thoughts are always correct, he will not try to become a fourth grader. He won't let go of his third grade level of thought because of his ego. At the same time, he believes his level is that of a sixth grader, with a sixth grader's knowledge and wisdom. He flaunts himself as a sixth grader, only to despair after running into the cold reality. In such despair, he may conclude that fate is cruel.

The wisdom that realizes your limitations should lead the way to straightening out your crooked mind, deepening your shallow mind, widening your narrow mind, and enlightening your darkened mind. By knowing that all human preconceived notions are mistaken and by surrendering them, your wisdom will grow.

We judge others with our preconceived notions of them from the past couple of years. How dangerous that is! Even though the other person has changed through time and space, and he or she is not the same person of a few years before, we still judge him or her with our preconceived notions. We do not know the present person at all. If you surrender your preconceived notions about another, as well as your notions of him or her from the present moment, you will become aware of the other's true identity.

HELL IS WHEN YOU HAVE A STRONG EGO

A person with a strong ego expects to be greeted first when he runs into a person of inferior status; otherwise, he feels ashamed. A person with a strong ego would also feel ashamed if his spiritual progress were slower than that of his fellow practitioners, especially if he had started the practice earlier than they. The stronger the ego, the more inferior he feels to an accomplished person. His face blushes from shame.

If you do not think of others as inferior and try instead to learn from them, if you do not think that you started spiritual practice earlier but instead believe that everyone is equal before Buddha, then you will find nothing of which to be ashamed. If you have practiced for, say, one year or for ten years, your brightness may be like a thirty-watt bulb or like a five-hundred-watt bulb. Next to the sunrise, however, both light bulbs would seem dim. Surrender the notion that you have been practicing longer than others, for in the sunlight all other lights are equal.

If your state of mind is one of serving Buddha, there is no suffering from a strong ego, because in reverent service the "I" is not allowed. In that moment of reverent service, everything is heavenly and bright, and the "I," which is only the physical body and suffering, cannot arise.

ONLY MY MOTHER

If you wished for your mother to be only your mother—to be neither your father's wife, nor your siblings' mother, nor your grandmother's daughter, nor your aunt's sister—if you wished for her to be only your mother, to take care of only you, then she would become miserable.

A child suffers the most when its parents' love is taken away by his or her newborn sibling. This is not only true with children. It is the same with a student who wants the sole attention of his teacher or an employee who desires the sole trust of his employer. By recognizing, however, that they are everyone's teacher, everyone's elder, everyone's Buddha, you will be able to cleanse the attachment to "only mine." When you cleanse the notion of "only mine," and when you realize that you are equal to all people, your wisdom tree will grow.

Only when you support your mother in her role as your father's wife, your grandmother's daughter, and your siblings' mother will she become greater than "only my mother."

We usually live our lives with the belief "I sacrifice myself for everyone else," rather than thinking "everyone else helps me." We believe that we pay taxes and go to tedious town meetings for our society and our nation. We focus on all the things we do for our families. With this attitude, many housewives begin to regret their lives when they reach old age. They ask for compensation for the youth they spent taking care of their family. Such people think that they are the only ones who have sacrificed for their families. They believe that only their lives are miserable.

If you are such a person, look back and see how lonely your life would have been without your husband and your children! Your husband was a guide through your rough life, a friend who talked to you during your spiritual hardships. Your children are not the burden of your life. See how meaningful and rich your life has been simply because they exist!

Usually parents think that they have to earn a living to raise their children, and they say, "I worked so hard to raise and educate my children." But an ancient sage once said, "Heaven gave a name to the grass when it created the grass, and food to humans when it created them." This means that a person is born with a certain collection of merit, and no matter what kind of household he is born into, the condition of his life really depends on that merit. These days there are too many children with too much worldly merit—their parents race around doing errands, providing for them. Then again, there probably are parents who live well because of their children's merit.

Looking back on the Vietnamese boat people who had no country, who died on small boats out of exhaustion, we are reminded of our country's service to us. Before dwelling on the idea that we pay taxes to run the country, think instead how grateful we should feel that our country protects us. Let's try and practice the grateful mind to the world that helps us.

DO NOT STOP PEOPLE FROM COMING TO YOU, NOR STOP THEM FROM LEAVING YOU

A bosallim had just begun the practice of reading the Diamond Sutra. Her oldest daughter was twenty-nine and the second oldest was twenty-seven. She said that their not being married was a big problem for her, and she let out a sigh as big as a mountain.

I told her to offer a won to Buddha by saying, "May my daughter meet a good husband so that they may serve Buddha well, barwon." And once again she diligently read the sutra, offered the won to Buddha, and practiced surrendering. One month later, her eldest daughter's marriage came through. Through the force of her won, which she had cultivated both in her previous lives and in this lifetime, the realities of her life changed.

Let's say that a person is invoking a won with the power of three hundred volts, and the person who tells him or her to make that won—the one who makes the decision—has a won with a power of one thousand volts. With the spark of their two wills coming together, they bring out the force of thirteen hundred volts. There is hardly anything that cannot be achieved with this kind of strength. In fact, since the end result of the wish is "to serve Buddha well," there is nothing that cannot be achieved. One thing to keep in mind is that you must trust the person who is making the decision for you to invoke the won, and you have to follow his or her directions. Only then will the won you invoke before Buddha be achieved.

When, in accord with her wishes, the bosallim had finally

married off her daughter, she felt so depressed and empty that she could not get up for three days. The bosallim's relationship with her husband hadn't been very good, and she had always depended on her eldest daughter for advice and friendship. She was used to discussing family problems with her. Upon finding a husband, however, the daughter left her mother without any regret. The mother grieved, "What can compensate me for my lost years? If I had known this would happen in the end, I would have used my life instead to follow the spiritual path and solve the problem of birth and death." She felt her whole life had been meaningless and in vain.

The aim of spiritual practice is to make your mind healthy. If you are accomplished in your training and help others with your mind, you will feel secure. But if you help others while your mind is still weak, your mind loses itself in the hope of a reward, and you become just an empty shell. From a healthy self, there is a healthy family, and from a healthy family there is a healthy nation.

When you do not block people from coming to you, when you do not stop people from leaving, and when your mind transcends both their coming and leaving, your spiritual practice is indeed accomplished.

F i v e

May You Accumulate
Much Merit

DON'T JUST HOPE TO BE WELL OFF, PLANT THE CAUSES TO BE WELL OFF

Everyone wants to be well off. However, we first must plant the causes of prosperity in order to achieve the desired effect. Always invoke a won to plant merit. If you then actually practice planting merit, you will be well off as a result.

If you invoke a won, the container that holds your merit will become bigger

Heaven bestows rain evenly, but a cup can only hold a cupful, a bowl can only hold a bowlful, and a washbowl can only hold a washbowlful. The water overflows if there is more rain than the vessel can hold. If you invoke a won to plant merit, your container of merit will grow. Invoking wons to plant much merit before Buddha means that you are making a vow to create opportunities by yourself—to actually plant merit—so that you may serve Buddha well.

Saving becomes merit

If our mentality is to be thrifty with the material goods that are the rewards of our precious labor, we plant merit. We should practice the thrifty mentality of conserving water, food, household furniture, and so on. We should also practice the mind of fixing items that are broken and of saving surplus goods to give them to those who need them.

Carefully saving your wages plants blessed fortune, too. Through doing so, your container of merit will grow. You do not accumulate merit by squandering money. If you spend money too freely, your good fortune will leave you.

You should not carelessly throw away food, such as rice. Often, housewives accumulate merit by serving food to their families, then nullify their merits by throwing away the leftovers. Whether it is water or electricity, if your mentality is that of regarding all things as valuable, if your mind is thrifty, then it immediately becomes merit.

Accumulate your merit aggressively

Merit is not something that you pray for. You have to aggressively plant merit, and you only receive as much as you have planted. You cannot give your merit to someone else, nor can you receive someone else's.

By transcending the boundary of self through the mentality of serving and sacrificing for family, neighbors, and society, you plant merit. The everyday practice of trying to help others with your giving mind becomes merit for your future.

Of course, by starting a project to serve Buddha—such as building temples, printing sutras, and so on—or by participating in such a project, you plant much merit, too. If someone accumulates merit from serving Buddha in whatever way, even after many incarnations he will be successful in the area in which he has accumulated his merit.

Sometimes, simply producing certain thoughts directly becomes merit for you: for example, revering Buddha with utmost devotion, wanting Buddha's bright Dharma to continue forever in samsara, revering all spiritual seekers, and wishing that they all attain enlightenment.

By cultivating your mind, you aid others with the radiance of your enlightenment. This becomes great merit, merit that makes the Buddha happy.

Prevent misfortune to retain your merit

Preventing misfortune is just as important as physically and spiritually planting merit. If a disaster strikes you, it can put a hole in the container that holds your merit. Just as water leaks through a bowl's crack, so too will your merit seep out.

For example, you could lose the merit that produces your material wealth through misfortune, and lose all your wealth through theft, fire, or illness. There are also many spiritual misfortunes that can obstruct your progress toward enlightenment. Such misfortune occurs as a result of bad karma accumulated in your past lives, or negative karmic ties with other people.

Therefore, if you read the Diamond Sutra day and night and surrender your arising minds well, without losing your mindfulness, the bad karma will gradually melt away and eventually be cleansed.

GREAT MERIT OF NO LIMIT

You might say that a person who owns a lot of material goods, who spends money like water, and who lives in an expensive house is blessed with much merit. However, you cannot call his or her merit "the great merit of no limit."

When someone has the great merit of no limit, he might not have much material wealth in ordinary times, but when the need arises he will be able to acquire anything he wants. If you possess much material wealth, you have to worry about taking care of it and protecting it. But with the great merit of no limit fulfilling your needs at any time, you do not have such concerns. With such blessed fortune, if you think that you need some warm clothes for winter, you get clothes in a few days. Even with food, if you demand what you need with your mind, it comes to you automatically. It is the same with daily supplies. If you generate the mind of want, in a couple of days, either someone will tell you where it is, or you will obtain it.

There was once a person whose health was weakening. He thought, "I will have to get some medicine chicks, and prepare them with ginseng." A few days after he had such a thought, someone brought him ten medicine chicks.

For some children, every time their parents want to do something for them, it just doesn't work out. But for others, as soon as their parents generate a wish to do something for them, it works out easily. For the children who have planted merit in their past, every time the parents want to provide something for them, it is immediately accomplished.

The great merit of no limit means one's blessed fortune never runs out. If there are no needy, poverty-stricken feelings in one's mind at all, one's face shines with merit. That person has cleansed every sense of poverty from his or her mind and has planted great merit before Buddha.

You plant the great merit of no limit when you practice such attitudes as utmost reverence to Buddha, a deep desire to repay Buddha's grace, joy about Buddha's realm of light, when you offer both your mind and body to Buddha to make him happy, and want to enlighten another's human nature to make Buddha happy, and so on.

SURRENDER EVEN YOUR MERIT

He who cultivates his mind is not greedy for merit. The merit that you plant will follow you anytime, anywhere, if you just pull at it like you would pull a yo-yo on a string.

If you generate the mentality of selfishly claiming your merit, your merit decreases. But if you surrender your merit to Buddha, you plant an even greater merit, and you imprint Buddha fully in your mind. At that instant, your mind comes closer to enlightenment, and your ego melts away.

We should surrender our intention to selfishly seek merit and recognition for our merit, and instead simply plant merit and cultivate wisdom.

YOU CANNOT GIVE YOUR MERIT TO SOMEONE ELSE, NOR CAN YOU ACCEPT SOMEONE ELSE'S MERIT

Once the Buddha went to accept the offering of a meal from a certain king. The greedy king wanted to keep the merit of the offering all to himself, so he announced that, from the day the Buddha arrived in his kingdom, anyone coming before the king would be punished according to the law of the land. And every day, in preparation for the Buddha's arrival, the king had his chefs make enough food to feed hundreds of people.

The day the Buddha arrived in the country with his disciples, no one went to tell the king because no one wanted to disobey the country's law. Even the chef would not tell the king for fear of punishment. He just made new meals every day and threw them away, making them again and again only to throw them away again and again.

As a result, the Buddha and his students had to starve for many days. When a merchant who was passing by the area heard the news, he offered them half of the five hundred bushels of oats that he had prepared for horse feed. Venerable Ananda went to the town with the oats and said, "The maiden who grinds these oats will become a princess in her next life."

When the ground oats were offered to the Buddha, the Buddha said, "Why didn't you say that she would become a Buddha in her next life? Becoming a princess is only one incarnation's merit, but if you had said that she would become a Buddha, she would have become a Buddha forever." Thus he pointed out

Ananda's error.

The Buddha asked the Venerable Ananda to try some food that the Buddha had just removed from his mouth. When Ananda tasted the food that had been chewed by the Buddha, he found it sweet and very delicious. Ananda asked, "Why are these oats so delicious?" The Buddha replied, "Food that enters the mouth of one who has planted much merit smells and tastes this way." The Buddha explained that this was the working of a person who had the power of merit.

You cannot give your merit to someone else, nor can you accept someone else's merit. In a family with many children, we sometimes see that material wealth and love are concentrated on a particular child. That is because he or she has planted more merit than the rest of his or her siblings. As the saying goes, "The shadow of Suyang Mountain stretches for eighty *li*." Even if only one person has planted merit in a family, many people still benefit from the power of that merit. However, one cannot give one's merit away. We see this is true in cases where the father dies and the family declines. Likewise, when a daughter with powerful merit gets married and moves away, her maiden household declines, but her newlywed household becomes well off.

There can be no blessed fortune where none has been planted. We should always put others before ourselves and constantly plant merit.

HOW TO SUSTAIN ONESELF IN THE FUTURE

Both humans and animals live with worries about what they will exist on in the future. Even wealthy people are not free from this psychological problem, because their minds are still poor.

Feeding oneself is a problem for everyone. Domesticated animals are absolutely loyal to their owners because their owners feed them. The debt of being fed is enormous. A cow struggles to avoid the slaughterhouse, but if its owner orders it to go, the cow will enter, reluctantly, because of its indebted mind. The cow eventually has to surrender its body, which has been raised on someone else's food, to the person who provided that food. The mind records all the actions of giving and receiving. In the end, it has to pay back its debt.

People live with this problem of the mind forever, worrying how they will survive in the future. This fear never ends. When you look into the mind of one who eats late at night, you will see that he or she overeats at that time because he or she is worried about being hungry in the morning. People crave higher positions because they want to be able to freely satisfy their basic desire—the desire for food. People bow before their superiors in the workplace. They grovel before powerful people. All these are actions of those who have not solved their worries about how they will support themselves in the future. Fear about how one will support oneself in the future arises not because there is no way of sustaining oneself, but because one's mind is poor.

PURIFY YOUR NEEDY MIND,
CULTIVATE YOUR PLENTIFUL MIND

Often, people who manage household budgets feel very constrained. They feel constrained by how much money they can spend in a month. They plan their budgets with a sense of being limited by monthly wages and respond to the world with the single notion of not having enough money. How desperate their minds are, living as they do with such a sense of deficiency!

People say that there are beggars with wealth and beggars without wealth. One who always has a sense of lack, though he is wealthy, is called the beggar with wealth. Whether you are wealthy or not, if your mind is deficient, you will constantly imprint deficiency and poverty in your mind. And if you imprint such notions in your mind without purifying them, you will become poor in this life and in the next. Even if you are not wealthy right now, if your mind is a wealthy person's mind, then your material wealth will become plentiful following your plentiful mind.

Usually, the face of one who has practiced a needy mind for one hundred days and the face of one who has practiced the plentiful mind for one hundred days are totally different. The power of merit and grace that radiates from the face of one with much merit is externally very different from that of the person with a needy mind.

Trivial thoughts accumulate one by one to form the foundation of your stability. You must surrender the needy mind and practice the plentiful mind.

If you have money in your pocket, even borrowed money, you feel confident when you go out. If your pockets are empty, your mind is constrained by such worries as "What if I need to spend some money?" or "What if I have to treat someone I meet?" Having enough money when you go out helps enlighten your mind.

Whenever our teacher sent us to buy something from the store, he always gave us plenty of money. Also, whenever anyone was looking for something, my teacher was ready immediately to give what was needed. He had all sorts of tools handy—a hammer, a wrench, a wire cutter, and so on. He even kept various types of nails handy that we did not immediately need. He told us to buy plenty of daily supplies, so we wouldn't have any sense of deficiency, and to arrange the necessary supplies neatly where we could easily see them.

Our teacher helped us to cultivate the plentiful mind and always told us to put it into practice.

BLACK PUPPY

Master Baek lost his parents early in his life, and so he lived with his grandmother. Because he was involved in the Korean Independence movement since his youth, he was considered a subversive character by the Japanese police, who relentlessly pursued him. Thus he was usually not at home, but wandering here and there until he finally left for Shanghai.

Master Baek's grandmother and sister were left at home. His grandmother was always worried, because there were only women living in the house. Consequently, she always hung Master Baek's clothes outside to dry and put out his shoes on the stepping stone even though he wasn't home. She worried that, if people thought the house was occupied only by women, they would try to take advantage of them or try to rob them.

One day, Master Baek's grandmother took half a sack of rice over to one of her poor neighbors. Since it was unusual for her to do something like that, Master Baek asked her why she gave them the rice. She said that she was being generous to them in order to prevent them from taking advantage of her household, for they might think that it was a wealthy household without any men. Master Baek, even in his youth, thought how great the merit she would have planted if she had just given the rice in hope that her neighbors would have a warm meal, instead of worrying about getting hurt by them.

Later, after Master Baek had returned from his study in Germany, he entered Geumgang Mountain to devote himself to the spiritual practice, determined to stay there for ten years.

But about eight years after he started his practice, he got a telegraph from home saying that he was to receive the family inheritance, for his grandmother had passed away. Even though it was an enormous amount of wealth, he did not go since it was during his retreat period.

The day after his ten-year retreat, he went back to his house in Seoul and saw that his grandmother had received a dog's body— she was reincarnated as a black dog and was guarding the house. In his Dharma lecture, Master Baek said that she had received this dog's body and had returned to guard the house because she died with the determination to protect her wealth.

She had lived in fear that someone might hurt her, so she clung to her wealth and guarded it until she died. Yet the outcome was, at most, being born as a dog.

If we do not cling to things, whether spiritual or physical, but surrender them instead to Buddha and give them away to others, it would benefit us even more. People, however, usually cannot do that.

PALACE GRANDMOTHER

Master Baek had an aunt who, because she was once a court lady at the palace, was called by her relatives the "palace grandmother." When she was nearing the end of her life, she wished to hand down her enormous wealth to Master Baek and kept sending people to inform him of her wish. But no matter how many times they came, Master Baek absolutely refused to inherit the wealth and did not even go to visit her.

Seeing this, one bosallim asked the enlightened Master Son Hye-jeong, "Why is Master Baek not even budging when many of his relatives, whom he rarely sees, come to give him this inheritance?" Master Son replied, "This is quite interesting." She said that Master Baek was trying to deliver his aunt.

The bosallim then asked, "How is he going to lead her to her salvation?" Master Son explained to her that Master Baek's aunt had conditioned a strong attachment to wealth all her life. Now Master Baek was trying to make her practice the mind of giving before she passed on to the next life, and that is why he was not going to see his aunt even though she wanted to give him everything. Master Son said to wait and see what would happen. Master Baek, of course, did not talk about any of this, but since Master Son was a living Buddha, she saw through Master Baek's mind.

Like Master Baek's aunt, most of us hoard our wealth all our lives for the "I." And when the moment of our death approaches, when we know that we can no longer take our wealth with us, we have to give our wealth either to "my" children, or to "my" close relative in order to ease the pain of not being able to take our money with us. Such is the greed of people who do not cultivate their minds, and that was why, since she had no children, Master Baek's aunt tried to give her fortune to her closest blood tie.

After a while, the visits from Master Baek's relatives stopped. Since he absolutely refused to receive the money, his aunt gave away all her wealth to her close relatives, distant relatives, acquaintances—even her kitchen maid and her cleaning boys. Eventually there was no more wealth to hand down to Master Baek, and there was no longer any need to send people to him.

One day Master Baek put a huge pile of large bills in a bag and went out to give it all to his aunt. She had been strongly attached to money all her life. Now that she had no money, her mind had become poor, and he wanted to save her from her own poverty-stricken mind. Although his aunt refused to accept the money, he told her to take it and almost forced her to keep it. If you die while imprinting the single notion of "having enough money" in your mind, you will have a lot of money in your next life.

For this reason, people who care for the elderly should always give them enough spending money. When you attend to an elderly person, you should not let him or her imprint the notion of "not having enough money" in his or her mind. Furthermore, if an elderly person is sick, you must do everything to cure his or her disease, for if he or she passes away with the mind-set of being sick, he or she will suffer from disease again in his or her next life.

After a few years, the bosallim became curious about what had happened to Master Baek's aunt, so she asked Master Son, "Did his aunt receive a human body?" And Master Son replied, "Of course. His aunt is a seven-year-old boy now, and though he is just a young child, he has a lot of money in his savings account."

An enlightened person uses various methods, depending on one's spiritual advancement or one's use of the mind at each moment, to lead beings to salvation. The enlightened person's measure is not what "I" can get out of it, but how I can make Buddha happy and be beneficial to all beings.

EARNING THREE TIMES YOUR WAGE

Expressing your healthy mind and body through your work is a joy of life, as refreshing as green grass. Every time you receive a paycheck, try to look back and see whether you have worked with the mindset of earning three times your wages for the company. If you can do this, you are a wise person, for you only receive the results of the causes that you have planted.

In Korea, I often see that workers at ironworks or people who do odd jobs at construction sites live in a cycle of poverty for their whole life. I wonder if this is because they live lives of incurring debts. For example, often when the workers at ironworks are welding pieces of sheet metal together, they cut up a full sheet when they could easily have used scrap pieces to do the same job. Often they use the resources too wastefully because the materials are not their own.

Some of the roofers I have seen are the same way. As they slate a roof, if the owner of the house did not provide them with generous snacks, they may intentionally make a hole in the roof so that the rain leaks in.

I wonder how they are going to cultivate their merit that way. Wouldn't that just increase their karmic debts and cause them to sink further into the cycle of poverty? The rule of causes and conditions is clear.

Many corrupt public officials during the first presidency of Korea also weren't true to their jobs. After they left the public sector, many of them started their own businesses with retirement pensions, but most of them failed. Since they had accumulated so much karmic debt to society while working in the public sector for thirty years, their businesses closed down to repay this karmic debt, just as water fills an empty pool. On the other hand, if someone were to diligently plant merit for thirty years, his planted merit would make his business prosperous.

Therefore, one who works with the mentality of earning three times his wages for the company is wise. For example, if you earn five thousand dollars but work with the intention of earning fifteen thousand dollars—five thousand for your employer, five thousand for tax and business expenses, and five thousand for yourself—then you will be successful in your workplace and in any society. Although you would not necessarily work like that, if you have such a mind-set, you would put detailed attention into each job you did, thus becoming more proficient and more productive.

In other words, you should be working with the mentality of an owner. One who has an owner's mentality would only be true to planting merit, whether others appreciate him or not. When you plant your merit in that way, no one but you receives that merit. There is no reason to claim any credit for doing a good job.

WHY MONEY IS NECESSARY

Modern society is based on its economic activities. Thus, one's economic well-being could be compared to the blood circulating in a human body. Just as blood is a basic element in the body, you have to have money to drive cars, buy food, meet people, buy clothes, get a house, get a cup of coffee, and so on. These days, life itself stops if you do not have money. Therefore, financial independence becomes a big part of spiritual independence. When I was studying at Sosa, the fact that we were self-sufficient with the money we earned from our farm definitely helped us to cultivate our confident minds.

It is said that money has its own eyes. In other words, you only earn as much money as you have planted merit. You should plant your merit by saving material goods with a thrifty mentality and by diligently working with the mentality of serving Buddha. Why plant merit? To provide food, clothes, and a house for the body that is serving Buddha, and to use the money in meaningful projects to serve Buddha.

Earning money is important, but spending it is also important. It would be a shame if you spent your money—hard-earned with merit—on seeking pleasure only.

Money is a tool—nothing more and nothing less—that lets people live like human beings. So, isn't it dangerous to think that money is happiness and the answer to your problems? If you always earned and spent your money with a humble mind and with the intention of serving Buddha, the merit vessel that holds your blessed fortune would become bigger and bigger.

There was an owner of a big conglomerate who returned all of his wealth to society before passing away. His son said to him, "Father, please hand down the company to me."

The billionaire, refusing him at once, replied, "I educated you up through college, and you have your own job. Why are you asking for your father's wealth?" The only wealth that he left to his family was a house he had bought for an impoverished nephew.

This billionaire realized the purpose of money and he practiced his own wisdom. Handing down our wealth to our children—because there is no way to take the fortune with us—is the greed of an uncultivated mind. The billionaire, however, started a firm to create jobs for many people in the 1950s, when times were tough. Such a person could be called a living bodhisattva.

According to Buddhism, a world will soon begin where material wealth is abundant, and life is comfortable due to the development of science and technology. This will be the period of "great merit of no limit," the world in which Tathagata Maitreya will appear. We should invoke a won to Buddha, wishing that everyone can be free from poverty and that everyone can have plenty of material wealth, so that they can serve Buddha well.

OFFERING A MEAL TO A DHARMA SEEKER

There was a temple called Yeonheung-sa located across from Sosa Monastery. The man who founded the temple was a lay follower named Wolgwang. He struggled for a long time in building the temple because he faced many obstacles along the way.

Seeing this, Master Baek told Wolgwang that if he fed anyone who entered his house for the next three years, the temple would be built. Just as he was told, after three years of practicing what Master Baek told him, the temple was built.

Eating is a fundamental preoccupation for sentient beings. From the perspective of receiving a guest, serving food is simply a basic courtesy, but for a human being it is even more fundamental than that. Regardless of the person, if food is served, his or her mind is soothed. It is as if the person is being served both with the food and with the warm mind of the host who serves it. At that moment, merit is accumulated in the host's mind.

There is a saying that the merit of serving a meal to one good person is bigger than serving meals to one thousand robbers, and the merit of serving a meal to one spiritual seeker is greater than the merit of serving meals to one thousand good people. It tells us of the rarity of people who cultivate their minds.

Spiritual seekers play the role of incarnations of Buddhas. With bright won and Dharma power, they brighten their surroundings. With their actions and Dharma lectures, they become guides for many people, calming their suffering minds. Because one way of showing reverence to them is materially, offering a meal is an expression of one's mind.

There is a story that explains why Mahakashyapa, one of the Buddha's disciples, was born into a rich family for hundreds of incarnations. Long ago, in one of his past lives, there was a terrible drought. After starving for a couple of days, he was able to get only a bowl of boiled millet. At that time, a pratyeka buddha came to beg for alms.

When Mahakashyapa offered up the bowl of boiled millet to Buddha, the pratyeka buddha gladly enjoyed the meal. Then the pratyeka buddha made a confirmation saying, "Every time you are born, you will become a rich man by this merit," and then he flew away into the sky. Because of this merit, Mahakashyapa was born into a rich family many times, including during the time of Shakyamuni Buddha.

Also, there is a saying, "Let an enlightened master become indebted to you unconditionally, whenever it is possible." If you do plant such merit, it is said that when you next meet the enlightened master, in whatever incarnation and wherever you are, you will be the first to be led to salvation.

OFFERING AND ACCEPTING DEVOTION

Every year, when summer came to Sosa, I would cut the grass around the monastery—one cart before noon and one cart after noon—to feed the cows. While I was cutting grass, I was usually able to find places where raspberries grew in abundance. Each time I discovered those fully ripened berries hidden in the forest, near the bank of a small stream, I couldn't have been any happier. By the mysterious stream bank, untouched by people, the luscious berries shone out red under the green bushes. The joy of discovering that delicious sight became even greater in my anticipation of serving them to my teacher.

On rainy days, because we couldn't work in the fields, we had some free time. At such times, I would put on my raincoat and go on an expedition to all the different valleys that I had noticed a couple of days before and fill empty baskets with raspberries. Since I was going to serve the berries to Master Baek, my mind and body were full of joy. It was my simple devotion that wanted to offer up everything to my teacher, who was enlightening my eternity.

Once, after I had been living at Sosa Monastery for four years, I returned home for the first time. After staying at home for about two weeks, I returned to Sosa and stopped by Haein-sa Temple on the way. Since it was autumn, the merchants were selling *darae* fruit. Hoping to offer them to my master, I bought some and carried them in a paper box. In those days, there were no highways, and after a long drive on unpaved roads, I reached

Sosa and opened the box of darae. Many of the fruits were squashed and looked unappealing. So I told the lady who was in charge of the kitchen that I could not offer the fruits to my teacher in such a condition, and I asked her to just throw them away. But she felt badly about throwing them away and put them on a tray to serve to our teacher. He enjoyed them all. My master had delightedly accepted my devotion, as well as my care in constantly worrying about the fruits being squashed while I was on the bus.

When enlightened people accept your offerings, they are not accepting the material goods, but rather your devotion and care. Master Baek gladly accepted the foods that were offered in reverence and devotion, but he rarely ate food offered otherwise. A poor bosallim used to save a little bit of money, taking a few cents from her grocery money each day, and she used it to buy fruit to offer up to Master Baek. The fruit she bought was not very good, but Master Baek enjoyed it all.

THE MENTALITY OF NOT BEING INDEBTED

When a gambler starts with twenty dollars and wins two hundred dollars, he becomes fiercely attached to that extra money as soon as it comes into his hands. So every time he loses some of that money, he becomes heartbroken. Everything except the original twenty dollars is free money, the loss of which should not upset him, yet he feels as if the extra money is the fruit of his honest labor. He thinks that the extra money is his and he laments losing it.

The mentality of seeking rewards without any effort is the nature of ordinary people. We wait for some distinguished man from the east to show up in due time to help us (a Korean expression for waiting for good luck to come by), like a person waiting under a plum tree for a ripe plum to fall into his mouth.

Nothing in the world is free, however. When someone gives something to you for free, he photographs the action of giving deep within his mind. When you receive something for free, you also impress that moment deeply in your mind, and, in your next life, you must pay back whatever you have received.

The mind that likes free things is that of a beggar and is an indebted mind. There is a saying that goes, "Even if you have only a crop of potatoes, if your mind-set is that of serving the potatoes to others, you have a rich person's mind. But, even if you have a crop of rice, which is more highly valued, if you have the mind-set of wanting to be served, you have the beggar's mind."

According to one of the sutras, Queen Mallika's five litter bearers were five monks whom Queen Mallika had served in her past life. It is said that, in order to repay the debt of the offerings that they had accepted from the queen, the monks had to spend their whole life carrying her carriage.

Also, long ago in India, monkeys would sometimes pick fruit and offer it to the ascetics who were devoting themselves to spiritual practice. As a result of such actions, when the monkeys were reborn as humans, the ascetics who had accepted the fruit were said to have often become their subordinates.

If you become the master of your economic and spiritual life and live with the giving, sharing mind, you can become enlightened.

A BOWL OF RICE

In order for a bowl of rice to get to your table, the heavens must have let the sun shine to grow the rice paddy and scattered just enough rain to wet the shoots. The earth must have opened its heart to let the rice spread its roots, and the wind must have blown cool breezes to ripen the crops. The whole process must be teeming with the sweat of the farmer who planted the rice in spring, pulled the weeds in summer, and harvested the crops in fall, and with the care of the one who made the warm bowl of rice, soaking it and boiling it.

Not only that but, in order for today's farming and the table in front of you to exist, there had to be vertical accumulation of technologies from numerous ancestors and traditions. Horizontally there were precious efforts by people in the modern age to produce farming tools, fertilizers, threshers, a rice mill, kitchen utensils, fuel, and so on. Therefore, how can you call a bowl of rice yours just because you bought it with your money?

Trace its history—in a bowl of rice, there is the grace of the entire human race and the whole universe. Thus, when you face a bowl of rice, you should first offer it up to Buddha, who is the guiding light of the human race and of nature. Be grateful to the ones who provided the meal, while invoking a won to serve Buddha well. Do this not only with food but also with clothes, books, and shoes. If you offer them all up to Buddha first and then use them, isn't that living in accord with the Dharma?

S i x

Reverence,

the Fragrance of Eternity

TREES IN FRONT OF THE BUDDHA HALL

When dark clouds storm in with their harsh rain and wind, all the insects and animals hide in their holes in the ground. Even the leaves curl up. But on a sunny day they all emerge, reaching out to the sun. The sun can be compared to Buddha. Reaching out to the sun may be the sprouting of faith that reaches out for brightness.

Once, I was standing behind the Buddha hall, in a nondual state of mind, completely empty of everything, just looking at the trees. As I watched, I saw the trees standing there with reverence, as if they were bowing their tops slightly toward the Buddha hall. I had just witnessed a split second when even the grass and trees solemnly took refuge in the bright Buddha hall.

NONDUALITY BASED ON UTMOST REVERENCE

It is said that to be a truly free person you must have the mentality "Kill the Buddha and kill the patriarchs." My guess, however, is that such a statement is only helpful for those who are at the level of Bodhidharma. In his Dharma lecture, Master Baek once said that, when Bodhidharma was practicing, Buddha's image often appeared in his visions. Bodhidharma tried to break the image with the thought, "Kill the Buddha and kill the patriarchs."

Such ideas can only be uttered at the level of one who is almost a living Buddha—such as Bodhidharma—at his special stage of practice. Wouldn't it be hazardous to advise ordinary people in this way? Bodhidharma must have made the statement in regard to the state of nondiscrimination, wherein one is not even attached to the Buddha. Yet even the state of nondiscrimination—nonduality—should be achieved on the basis of utmost reverence if it is to be enlightening.

In the mind that is full of ego, a claim that one has reached the nondiscriminative state is merely empty words. It is a karmic hindrance. Since there is no "I" in absolute reverence, however, everything you do with that reverence naturally becomes nondual. Your mind should be one of unconditionally folding your hands and bowing the moment you hear the word "Buddha," so that you can plant merit and become enlightened. Isn't trying to become enlightened "by yourself," without any reverence, just practicing your ego? Trying to become enlightened through your ego is like trying to prepare a bowl of rice with sand.

Still, you should neither see Buddha as the object of reverence, nor "I" as a separate subject of reverence. In the place of absolute reverence, there is no "I"; therefore, there is nothing to be distinguished. Thus, without picturing Buddha as an object of reverence, it may be best simply to lower ourselves before the mind that reverently calls out, "Lord Buddha" and, facing that reverent mind, practice the mindset of being in the presence of Buddha.

SURRENDER WITH REVERENCE

It was the year I turned twenty-eight at Sosa. One day, after finishing the morning practice, I headed back to my room. Remembering that there was something I needed to ask my master, I turned around, and on my way back I perceived an energy that completely filled the sky, incredibly solemn and bright. It was just before dawn.

That fully bright energy was tremendously solemn and heavy. The moment I perceived it, I gasped as though I was being smothered by something, as if the universe were falling on my chest. It was overwhelming. I stared blankly into the sky and probably recited *Mireukjon Yeoraebul* in my mind.

Immediately I went to my teacher and asked him about my experience. He explained, "You have just perceived the Dharmakaya (Dharma-body Buddha). It shows that the ego has melted away. When this happens, you should fold your hands and bow down halfway saying, 'I will serve you well.' Did you do that?" When I told him that I had not, he told me to do so right away and personally showed me how.

He said that if you do not practice your reverence in ordinary times, you will run into trouble in such a situation. The moment you witness the Dharmakaya, if you generate reverence to the Buddha by saying, "I will serve you well," you will advance even further in your spiritual practice. But if you do not generate reverence, but stand stiff, with the attitude of "I am as much of a Buddha as you are," or with the attitude of "Kill the Buddha, kill the patriarchs," the bright energy of Dharmakaya will strike down your ego. When that happens, you will change your body in three days. For example, there was once a person at Sosa Monastery who perceived the Dharmakaya in his past life while practicing Zen. But he said that, since he did not pay reverence to the Dharmakaya, he was punished by it.

Each time your discriminating mind calms, you witness radiance. This means that you are perceiving the Buddha, for there isn't anywhere on earth where Tathagata Maitreya has not cultivated his virtues. He remains as white radiance all over the universe.

However, you should not keep such concepts as "Dharmakaya" or "radiance" in your mind. Even Buddha is no longer "Buddha" when you enclose him in your mind—Buddha becomes only your mind's discriminative notion.

There once was an accomplished master who had never met a fully enlightened one, so he always held a preconceived notion of Buddha as bright radiance. He lived his whole life with that preconceived notion, unable to surrender it. When Master Baek searched for that monk with his wisdom-eye after he had passed away to see where he went, Master Baek found him trapped in light that looked like white pottery. Since the monk pictured Buddha as radiance in his mind and directed his mind toward it, he could only end up sitting inside a luminous and cloudy light.

As this master's fate illustrates, it becomes a problem if you draw anything in your mind. You should surrender even the discriminative notion of who Buddha is and surrender the act of surrendering. No matter what type of discriminating mind it is, you should surrender it in that short moment of nonduality and

nonwandering thoughts, when you call out with all your heart
and with reverence, "Buddha!"

KING ASHOKA

The following events took place while Buddha was residing in Jeta Grove, the garden of Anathapindika's park in Shravasti.

One day, as usual, Buddha entered the city of Shravasti to collect alms with Ananda. They encountered some children on the road, playing happily with mud. They pretended that it was treasure or food and piled it up in a mud storehouse.

One of the children saw the Buddha coming his way from afar. He was filled with joy at Buddha's holy appearance, so he wanted to make an offering to Buddha. But there was nothing to offer him besides the mud treasures and mud crops.

Since he was so tiny, he asked another child to let him climb up on his back. He offered up one fistful of mud crops from the mud storehouse to the Buddha. Seeing the child's devotion and kindness, the Buddha lowered his bowl to receive the offering. The Buddha gave the mud to Ananda, saying, "Plaster my room with this mud."

After they had returned to the temple, Ananda plastered a corner of Buddha's room with the mud. It disappeared quickly for it was such a small amount. Ananda told the Buddha, "I plastered a corner of your room with the child's mud, Lord." Buddha, with a joyous look, gave this Dharma lecture to Ananda:

"Ananda, that child has offered a fistful of mud with reverence to Buddha, and covered a corner of my room with it. From this merit, in his next life, he will become the king of a great nation, and he will be called Ashoka. The children who were playing with him will become his ministers and rule the nation together. They will uphold the three jewels of Buddha, Dharma, and Sangha, make offerings to many, spread Buddha's relics everywhere, and build eighty-four thousand stupas to greatly propagate the Buddhadharma."

VENERABLE SHARIPUTRA

Once, when the Buddha was first spreading the Dharma, one of his monks was walking on a certain street, exuding his Dharma power. Just then, Shariputra was passing by that area, and he was greatly impressed by the way the monk carried himself. So Shariputra went up to him and asked, "Who is your teacher?"

The monk replied, "My teacher is Gautama Siddhartha."

Shariputra asked again, "What is his teaching?"

"He teaches that everything arises from causes and conditions, and everything ceases when the causes and conditions cease."

On hearing such an enlightening Dharma lecture for the first time, a great admiration for Shakyamuni Buddha arose in Shariputra's mind. So, he asked the monk to lead him to the Buddha, and taking his friend Maudgalyayana with him, they immediately joined the Buddhist order.

From then on, the Venerable Shariputra always paid reverence to the monk who introduced him to the Buddha. Because that monk was practicing in the East, the Venerable Shariputra never slept with his feet in that direction.

SNOW AND STAR

Once I cultivated a desolate mountain slope at Sosa. Besides the approximately three acres of land that we farmed, we also cultivated about three acres on a mountain face to create a pasture for cows.

Normally, due to our busy schedule, I would not have even dreamt of pursuing such a venture, but I started the project in winter, when I still had some free time. I put the rocks that were scattered all over the mountains and fields in my rack and placed them in the troughs between the planted pastures. Despite the freezing weather that had caused the mercury to drop to fifteen degrees below zero, and even in the middle of a blizzard, I made spare time to clear the mountain by myself.

As I was working, I surrendered all sorts of mental obstacles—such as cold weather, wind, and snow—with a loud recitation of *Mireukjon Yeoraebul*. When at last my practice seemed to be continuing smoothly, I saw my aged master in the distance walking up through snow falling so heavily that it almost blocked one's vision. He had come all the way up there for the chance to strengthen my practice of surrendering. When an enlightened master gives such a confirmation at the moment Dharma awakens in you, your practice becomes stronger.

I could only be grateful to him. Overwhelmed with deference, I wasn't even able to greet him properly. I just worked with the rack on my back while continuing my practice. He silently looked at me for a while, then, after invoking a won for me, he slowly walked back down the hill. Seeing him carefully walk down the snowy hill, I folded my hands and bowed while invoking a won, "May I be able to attend our teacher well, so I can serve Buddha well."

One day, when Sosa was entirely white with snow, I came down from my room around two in the morning to clear a path. I was worried that our teacher might slip while he was going to the bathroom. Unbeknownst to me, my master had already come outside, aware that I was hard at work clearing away the snow.

While standing there, he gave an incredible Dharma lecture on the mysterious realm of enlightenment until 4:30 in the morning. The moment I heard my master's own voice telling me about the mysterious, secret realm of Buddha, and his own experiences with things that one can hardly even imagine, my reverence and won of admiration toward Buddha blossomed more greatly and clearly than the white glimmer of the snow, the pure vitality of daybreak, or the early morning sky.

As the Dharma lecture was about to end, bright stars sparkled in the blue sky of dawn.

VISITING THE MASTER AT DAYBREAK

When I was running a business, I would take the first bus once a week from the Seoul train station to Inchon at 4:10 a.m. to visit my master at Sosa and to practice there. Those times, reverently beholding his compassion and listening to his Dharma lecture, my heart was filled with awe and radiance.

My memory of visiting him on one cold winter day is especially vivid, and I am transported once more back to that time.

It is the day before I am supposed to go to Sosa. I go to the grocery store, and I pick the best and the freshest fruits to offer my teacher. When I wipe the fruits with cautious hands, three times each with a wet towel and a dry towel in order not to bruise them, the fragrance of reverence and joy, thicker than that of the fruit, seems to permeate the entire town.

In the middle of my reciting the sutra, the siren sounds at 4:00 A.M. to end the curfew. As I go to his place with the fruit under my coat and suit, embracing them with my body heat, since they might freeze in the cold weather of minus ten degrees, my mind is that of a seeker whose whole life is surrendered to Buddha and to my master.

As I walk the streets with a cool head and a warm heart, the hazy white radiance, as peaceful as the fog of early morning, seeps into every corner of my tranquil mind. This bright mind, free of its body, is headed only to the enlightened master, to the place of refuge. The won, made before Buddha, of a wayfarer who is awakened to the importance of his master must have been realized.

The first bus arrives at the corner of Sosa in no time. When I get off the bus, the light from the distant white cross on the top of Shinangchon village comes into sight, and the cold morning air seeps into my body.

As I picture myself reflecting on the wisdom of an enlightened master, I hurry to his house. The karmic hindrances that I have surrendered well, thus strengthening my practice, and the karmic hindrances that have escaped from me all come to my mind clearly. As I reflect on those moments, my tense mind surrenders them even harder by reciting *Mireukjon Yeoraebul*.

When I arrive in front of the gate, where a carving of the Diamond Sutra passage "Thus ye shall view" hangs, the master is already waiting for me, as if he knew I was coming.

"You're here! The door lock is frozen from the snow. I'll bring some hot water." My teacher's voice is as rich as a thick iron chain being dragged across a cement floor.

He brings some hot water with a dipper to melt the ice and to open the door for me. Under his warm winter hat, a look of delight settles on his radiant face, a look full of compassion. He is wearing a thick winter jacket, gray wool pants, and shoes lined with artificial fur.

After passing through the long white corridor, I enter the Buddha hall. There is bright energy all around, brighter than the fluorescent light reflected by the white walls of the Buddha hall. The warmth of the room thaws my freezing hands and cheeks.

My teacher enters through the back corridor, and after giving me a cushion to sit on, he sits on a cushion with a pleased look on his face. When I bow down to him three times, he invokes a won for me. With the sound of his energetic Dharma voice, the past week's pain and suffering melts away, and strength surges through my body.

When he tells me to practice surrendering while kneeling but keeping my hips and back straight and goes into the next room, I place my cushion about thirty centimeters away from the wall and start reciting *Mireukjon Yeoraebul.* I practice surrendering while gazing at the wall.

My wish to be with him and listen to him speak is even greater than my wish to practice. So when I see him going to the next room, I am a bit disappointed. Being aware of my mind, he says, "Well, then," and sits down again to give me a Dharma lecture.

Twenty minutes into the practice, the pores on my back start stinging. A little longer into the practice, the palms of my folded hands and my back start becoming warm, and soon my whole body is sweating. At that moment, my body and mind couldn't possibly have felt any better. After I sweat, my master finally comes out and tells me to sit down, and I finish my practice.

Sometimes, on the bare floor, I practice surrendering for about four hours in this kneeling position, but he still does not come out of his room. At such times, my body becomes soaked with sweat. Also, since I have been practicing with a loud recitation, my voice is strained and hoarse for about three of those four hours. But when I continue my practice, my voice suddenly bursts open and becomes even clearer than before. My whole body is tired, and my knees are numb, beyond the point of sensing any pain, but my body and mind are refreshed. I feel as if I could fly away.

During practice, all the memories of recent painful or regrettable incidents come to my mind. I feel exactly the way I felt when those incidents happened. This sickens my heart and clouds my mind. As the practice goes on, those painful feelings become thinner and lose their color until my mind becomes light and calm.

Gradually, as the remaining heavy feelings that have not yet been surrendered are finally surrendered, my heart calms and my mind is focused. At that point, I am in a natural state of no thought, no action. In that state, if I want to know the answer to a question, I recite *Mireukjon Yeoraebul* to that question and an answer comes to me. Sometimes, if my practice of surrendering continues well, I even perceive the white radiance.

When my master comes back, I end my practice and ask him the questions that occurred to me during practice. He explains them to me one by one. If there are things that I can't understand, he tells me to constantly surrender that sense of not being able to understand.

He then gives a Dharma lecture for many hours. The realm of his Dharma lecture is simply bright. Master Baek has an awareness that penetrates through the past, present, and future of all things and beyond. He lectures about the physical attributes of people who attended Shakyamuni Buddha, the Dharma lectures of the Buddha, the depth and shape of certain valleys of the Kun Lun Mountain, and the plants that live within that valley. He lectures as if he is actually there. He also lectures on the law behind the creation of the universe, the destiny of nations and the world, and deep questions of physics. When he is asked about any person, he knows his or her face, mind, and future in detail.

His is the mind that knows everything due to surrendering all the things he doesn't know. Though he has never read about them or heard about them, he just knows them. I am simply amazed at how he knows everything. Each time I come to study with him, he lectures on something new. He does not teach us from his memory. Depending on the people he teaches, he uses the most adequate answers to suit each person. No matter how unfamiliar our questions are, there is no question that he does not answer from his bright mirror of wisdom. He knows everything by surrendering the discriminative notion of not knowing.

Since my mind is reverently directed to him as I hear his Dharma lecture, I receive his radiance in full. After meeting with him, the energy I receive from him lasts for a whole week.

Around 10 A.M. we have breakfast at the same table. Sometimes there is no one working in the kitchen and he says, "I'll get the breakfast ready. You just continue your practice here." Out of deference, I reply, "I'll get the breakfast ready, sir."

Then he says, "No, it's okay. Since you're unfamiliar with the kitchen, I'll go and prepare the meal."

It is a simple menu. Whenever he eats kimchi, he starts eating from the outer, blue part of the cabbage that has already lost its taste. In the tranquility of the meal, there is only the occasional sound of spoons clanking. It is a moment when even the sense of taste has been surrendered, so we finish the meal without any notion of taste. We are simply full.

Around noon, I say, "Master, since the briquette fire at the store should be nearly out, I have to go back now."

When I get up to leave, he says, "Here, take the lit briquette with you," and laughs cheerfully. He tells me to practice surrendering continually. After I give him three bows and leave, he comes out to the door as usual to see me off with his carefree laughter, like that of a loving grandfather.

WHEN YOU GIVE THE DIAMOND SUTRA

You should only give the Diamond Sutra to someone who will definitely read it, for if the person who receives the sutra despises it or steps on it, that person will get stepped on by someone else. And when that happens, the person will then try to get his revenge on the one who gave him the sutra. Therefore, how can we not be careful?

Once, I gave copies of the Diamond Sutra to my nephews, who believed in a different religion. These children, who were in high school and middle school, could not have known the importance of the sutra. I gave them the sutras only because I wished to do so.

Later, by chance, I told Master Baek what I had done. He said that they would trample on my head. I asked him why, and he said that they would receive karmic retribution for belittling the sutra, and, since my nephews would receive this retribution because of me, they would step on my head. He said that when you give a sutra to someone get two or three confirmations that they will read it and give it only to a person who asks for it.

Once, I also left about four hundred midsized Diamond Sutras at a follower's home. I had been worried that I had no place to enshrine the sutras, so she suggested enshrining them at her house. A couple of days after I had enshrined them, a mischievous boy of that household exchanged them for candy at a junkshop. When I found this out, I was so shocked that I almost fainted.

Even after searching all the junkshops in Pohang, Daegu, and Busan, I could not find the sutras. I searched the shops in Pohang again carefully and found three bundles of one hundred each. But still I could not find the remaining bundle. A few days later, the boy who had sold the sutras was in a train accident. It was summertime, and he was sleeping on top of the railroad tracks when a train ran him over. He was hurt badly, but his limbs were not cut off. It was the worst experience. I told my master about the incident and was scolded by him again.

In the Sutra of Karmic Causality, there is a verse about a person becoming a hunchback due to the karmic retribution of throwing the sutra on the ground. Also, in the Diamond Sutra, it is written that if you enshrine the Diamond Sutra and study it well, Buddha sees this, and the bright force that surrounds the area will protect the place where the Diamond Sutra is enshrined.

The Diamond Sutra is the sutra that contains Buddha's mind. It is a precious teacher that makes us reach toward Buddha's enlightenment and helps us to learn and practice that enlightenment. Aside from worrying about karmic retribution, if we simply enshrine the sutra well and give it to others wisely, we will develop the proper attitude of one who studies Buddhadharma.

Seven

May We All Serve Buddha Well, Barwon!

MAY WE ALL SERVE BUDDHA WELL, BARWON!

Ordinarily, we make offerings to Buddha and pray for ourselves and for the health of our family, happiness, academic achievements, success in business, and cures from illnesses. I suppose if you prayed fervently enough, these wishes could come true for you. But, from a spiritual practitioner's point of view, such prayers can become a problem because, if you keep practicing the mentality of begging from Buddha, you may very well end up weakening yourself. The more you beg from Buddha, the more your mind becomes that of a beggar. The more you depend on Buddha, the weaker your mind becomes.

There is a difference, for example, between saying, "Buddha, please make so and so pass the entrance exam" and saying, "May so and so pass the entrance exam so that he can serve Buddha well, barwon!" Though the content is the same, the prayers differ both in their intentions and in their results.

The first prayer bears the mentality of hoping to obtain what one wants from Buddha. Such an attitude can turn into resentment of the Buddha if one's wish doesn't come true. But the latter mentality is one of wishing for something in order to serve Buddha well. Such a mindset is righteous and brave.

More aggressively, one can invoke wons such as, "Lord Buddha, may I surrender all my arising minds and eternally enlighten this one mind, so that I can make Buddha happy, barwon!" or, "I do not have the ability to make Buddha happy right now, but with diligent effort, I vow to make Buddha happy, barwon!" or, "By helping to spread Buddha's bright Dharma to many people, may I serve Buddha well, barwon!" The person who invokes these wons practices a brave and enlightened mind.

Since the proper mentality is to serve the omnipotent Buddha—who completely fills the universe—with this mind, how brave and grand the basis for such an intention is! By performing such virtuous deeds, one accumulates merit in one's mind and awakens wisdom. Therefore, the brightest and greatest won that we can make is the won to serve Buddha well. Becoming one with this won and always serving Buddha is the great path that leads to enlightenment.

Let's continually invoke wons. For everyone you run into, invoke a won. "May this person awaken faith and devotion so that he or she can serve Buddha well, barwon!" For every incident you face, "May this thing be resolved brightly to serve Buddha well, barwon!" Even when looking at the sky and the trees, pray, "May nature awaken faith and devotion to serve Buddha well, barwon!"

BUDDHA WORK IS BASED ON WON

Goals should be pursued with a natural flow instead of an artificial force. The basis for such a flow is the power that comes from making persistent wons. If you pursue a goal and become involved before the time and atmosphere are ripe, you will clash with the existing atmosphere and create discord and dissonance. On the other hand, if you constantly invoke wons and the power of your won is ripe, you will see that the atmosphere becomes bright and the goal is accomplished naturally.

If you say, "I'll do it in such and such a way," then the action is directed at and concluded in you. But if you say, "May it be done in such and such a way to serve Buddha well, barwon!" then your action is directed instead toward the radiance of the Buddha and the work will end up being the Buddha's work.

EVERY MOMENT WE FULFILL OUR WISHES, YET EVERY MOMENT WE COMPLAIN

A certain bosallim made a won saying she wanted nothing except an intelligent and good-natured son-in-law. Because she had been practicing devoutly for three years, her wish came true, and she married off her daughter.

As it happened, her new son-in-law had also been invoking a won to marry the daughter of a wealthy family, a family that was also devoutly Buddhist. The bride's household was one of the wealthiest in the city, and the young man's family was so poor that they did not even own a television set. Nonetheless, he had paid his way through Seoul National University's Law School, and he was studying for his bar exam. Since the bride's mother had to convince her husband to permit the marriage, she lied to him, saying that the young man's family was well off while secretly paying the groom's wedding expenses herself. For three years now, she has been providing their living expenses while her son-in-law studies for his bar exam.

One day, she came to me and complained about her lot, saying that she didn't know why she had to face such trouble. People fulfill their wishes every second of their lives, and they complain every second of their lives. When she was invoking the won, if she had said, "a son-in-law who is well off and also intelligent" instead of saying, "nothing except," the situation would have been completely different. She invoked such a

141

won because she was unwise. Her won came true, but she still complained.

One should always invoke a bright won, a complete won, the result of which is "to serve Buddha well, barwon!"

THE GOVERNOR OF GYEONGSANG PROVINCE

During the Joseon dynasty in Korea, the governor of Gyeongsang Province had his office in Andong. In a town in Andong, there lived a young couple and their six-year-old son. On the day that the governor of Gyeongsang Province was to arrive for his post, the town held a festive procession with much fanfare, and when the six-year-old boy saw the procession, he said to his father:

"Father, when I grow up, I am going to become the governor of Gyeongsang Province, too."

And his father said, "You cannot become a government official because you are a person of low birth."

On hearing this, the child was shocked. He began to wither and weaken, and eventually he passed away. The father was so distraught that every year he made an offering for his son on the anniversary of the night he died.

Fourteen years later, a twelve-year-old governor of Gyeongsang Province came to office. While touring many different places in Andong, he found a familiar town.

For many years, on the seventh day of every eleventh lunar month, he had dreamed of a small stream that flowed through a thick, old pine forest. Past the stone bridge by the stream, there was a thatched house just outside the town, and inside the brushwood gate, there were two date trees standing in front of the well near the house. In his dream, he used to open the brushwood gate and go into the house, where he was served a great deal of food. He had had that exact dream the day before, and now he stood in the very same town.

He opened the brushwood gate of the house with the two date trees standing in front of the well. A man who seemed to be slightly less than forty years old came out of the room and saw the governor. Next, a lady came out of the kitchen, having heard someone open the brushwood gate.

The twelve-year-old governor of Gyeongsang spoke first. "Was there an offering in this house last night, by any chance?"

The couple looked at each other in surprise. The husband answered, "Yes! There was an offering here last night. But how did you know that, sir?"

"Last night, I dreamed of coming here and eating a lot of food. But who is the offering for?"

The man replied, "It was an offering for our son, but..."

The governor asked, "Why were you making an offering for your son?"

Since the young governor was curious, they told him the full story of their son, who had died fourteen years before. While listening to the story, the governor's heart overflowed with emotion. He held their hands tightly and said, "You must be the father and mother of my past life." With that, the governor collapsed on the spot and died without a word.

Fourteen years before, the six-year-old child was shocked and had died with a wish unfulfilled. The spirit was born as the son of a princess in order to become the governor of Gyeongsang. At age twelve, he had begged the king, his maternal grandfather, to let him become the governor. As soon as he had fulfilled his wish, he changed his body and passed away just like that.

SENTIENT BEINGS LEAVE THE WORLD AFTER FULFILLING THEIR WISHES

Sometimes, when people finally gain wealth and begin to enjoy themselves after having led a poverty-stricken life, they pass away. Their relatives lament, for the deceased did not even get to enjoy life once it finally turned around for them. Because such a person's sole wish is to become wealthy, when that wish finally ripens and he is actually able to live well, his mind wears out completely and he dies. It is the same as becoming totally exhausted and not being able to get up after finishing an important, anticipated event.

There was a student who, after ten years of hard work to receive his Ph.D., died in a German airport on his way back to Korea. His sole wish was to earn the Ph.D. degree, but when he finally received the degree, he felt, "Did I go through all that just to receive this piece of paper?" The sense of futility made him let go of his mind, and he died.

There is, however, a way to live longer in such situations. If you make such wons as "May I be freed from poverty to serve Buddha well, barwon!" or "May I receive a Ph.D. to serve Buddha well, barwon!" in ordinary times, you will live well in order to serve Buddha. It is because people have no other wish than to be well off or to receive a Ph.D. that they just end with the fulfillment of their wish.

If you do not know how to invoke a won, after you fulfill your wish, you should produce the mentality to do more meaningful things through the wish that has been realized. Leaving the world after fulfilling one's wish is the way of all sentient beings. One who leaves the world after having served Buddha well is fortunate.

E i g h t

Absolute Freedom
Is Loneliness

ABSOLUTE FREEDOM IS LONELINESS

Let's say someone is on a ship, with plenty of food, drifting in the middle of an ocean by himself. Since there is no one he has to deal with, all is peaceful for a while. But the depth of loneliness arising from within becomes too deep and dark for him to climb out. It is as painful as death itself, for his inner world, filled with loneliness, is withering away.

Human beings are social animals that cannot live alone. Thus, the loneliness of drifting alone in the middle of an ocean is horrible mental torture. We can see why serious criminals are put in solitary cells—such treatment is mental abuse that leaves no physical scar.

Loneliness is the biggest problem that every living being has to solve. The biggest burden for people who cultivate their minds is freeing themselves from loneliness. If you are busy, your mind is absorbed in your work and does not have time to become lonely. If you were a traveler, however, eternally walking alone in a desert, how desperate you would be for people and conversation!

A human being might be seen as a single fir tree under a sky of loneliness, reverently folding its hands to the sun from time to time, while being rained on by the shower of ignorance. With its branches boldly stretched toward the sun, with its sturdy roots that do not shake in the wind, it gratefully seeks the rays of sun that shine down on it. It is like the spiritual seeker looking up to the unknown state called Buddhahood.

Devoting yourself to spiritual practice means picking out and cleaning the seed that is covered with the shade of loneliness and darkness. The pain of purifying loneliness and the bliss of being freed from it are special states understood only by those who have cleansed loneliness from their minds. If one is lonely neither in a crowd nor in the deep mountains, one is an able person who knows how to enjoy absolute freedom.

WHEN YOU ARE FREED
FROM LONELINESS

When I first entered Sosa, I was often all by myself in the huge monastery. The other practitioners had not yet come, and my mind was full of loneliness.

During that time, one of the things Master Baek repeatedly told me was a story about his days in public service. When he went to department stores, the salespeople would say, "Sir, you must have many grandchildren, right?" and they would recommend that he buy things for his grandchildren. He said that he appeared to have many grandchildren because he did not feel any loneliness and did not give out any sense of loneliness. He often said that one's spiritual practice is complete when one finishes purifying all the loneliness from one's mind. Because I was only twenty-six-years old, and because I had just started my practice, such lectures did not make much sense to me. I wondered why he told me these stories so often.

He said that people who are freed from all the emotions of male-female relationships, including sexual desire, do not emit any odor from their bodies. People who are liberated from such desires give out a fragrant scent.

Much of literature, music, and art deals with the subject of loneliness. Loneliness is rooted in the desires of the flesh, the attachment to one's body. The creative work of one who has not cleansed his or her desires of the flesh is usually mixed with greed, anger, and arrogance. However, when Buddha is present within one's mind there is no loneliness. One who has purified the root of loneliness does not suffer from being alone.

Master Baek said that in the music of Handel and Bach, for example, the desires of the flesh are less evident. This is probably because their music has a brightness that reveres the glory of God—the music comes from an attitude of worship and devotion. The words to popular songs are often about unfulfilled love, longing, loneliness, and resentment. Loneliness, a desire of the flesh, is what all living beings must surrender to their very roots, until they finally attain Buddhahood.

KEEP A DISTANCE THE LENGTH OF
A BULL'S REIN WHEN YOU GET TO KNOW
SOMEONE

If you go too near a bull, you can either be hurt by the bull's sharp horns or receive a friendly gesture and be slobbered on by his wet tongue. On the other hand, if you stand too far away, you'll lose your grip on the rein, and he will run away. A runaway bull ruins vegetable fields, and when you try to catch him, he always runs out of reach when you approach. Thus, the length of a bull's rein is the perfect distance within which to control the bull.

Getting acquainted with people is the same way. If you become too close to someone without having freed yourself from your ego, you will find the other's flaws first. Without realizing that the flaws that you see in the other person are flaws in your mind, you criticize the other person. The other person is the same way. He or she judges you with his or her own flaws.

There is a saying, "When kids become too close to each other, tears come out of their eyes." When you are too close to someone without the ability to control your mind, since your mind is full of ego, your relationship will be unstable. For example, when you like someone, you want to give that person everything you have, even your own flesh, but if you suddenly come to dislike the person, the poison of murderous hatred rises up in you. In the name of friendship, we practice a solicitous mentality, yet ask for things in return for our friendship.

In this way, the darkest spot is right under the lamp. If you're too close to someone, you can't see his virtues. Likewise, if you are too far from him, you cannot see either his virtues or his limitations. One who cultivates the mind should be able to see others as Buddhas. When you are determined to see others as incarnations of the Buddha, you will feel reverence and sheer joy arising from your heart.

WARMTH IS WITHIN BUDDHA'S BOSOM

When children reach adolescence, they start disobeying and rebelling against their parents. This is painful, especially for the mother, because her children defy her after she has nurtured them with all her mind and body. From the children's point of view, however, it is perfectly justified. When they were young they could not survive without their parents, so they had to obey them. Now that they are older, they awaken to the instinct that tells them that they do not need their parents anymore.

At this point, a wise person would say, "I guess this is a sign that they have grown up." He or she would not be disappointed. But parents usually say, "How could they do this to me after all I have done for them?" and demand recognition for their efforts. This is painful for everyone.

Once, an enlightened master went to a cremation site. He saw two children, a nine year old and a ten year old, crying their hearts out after having cremated their mother. When the master looked into their minds, he saw that they were thinking, "How are we going to survive now?" Rather than crying out of sorrow or love for their mother, they were crying because they felt hopeless about their own future. Most people consider their own needs first in this way. When you look at such incidents as parents and children suing each other and killing each other for money, siblings fighting with each other, husbands and wives becoming enemies after a divorce, and close friends not speaking to each other because of their conflicting interests, relationships between human beings seem so heartless. This is because everyone tries to live only for himself or herself.

Most of us fiercely feed our egos by putting "me" before my parents, "me" before my siblings, "me" before my wife, "my interest" before that of the neighbors and the country. This is the innate nature of all beings.

Whom can we trust and on whom can we depend? If two porcupines were to hug each other out of love, they would pierce each other with their spines. Likewise, we should understand that relationships between beings who still have an ego are usually like porcupines hugging one another. Therefore, we might as well condition our minds to be broad and generous, so that we can hug the people who hurt us. We should condition our minds to be healthy, so that even if we are disturbed by shocks such as betrayal, we can overcome the pain.

The Diamond Sutra states, "All conditioned things are like a dream, a dew drop, a masquerade, or a bubble." Our world is this way and so too are our lives. One should not lose one's mind to a person or to work. Only while looking up to Buddha should we surrender our rising thoughts and emotions, moment after moment.

AN EMBROIDERED PHOENIX MIGHT BE SEEN, BUT THE NEEDLE TIP CANNOT BE SEEN

There is a saying, "An embroidered phoenix can be seen, but the tip of the needle that created the phoenix cannot be seen." How many tiresome days must someone have worked with that weary needle! We might call this the beautiful virtue that does not display the hardship of blood and tears, but only shows the grandeur of the phoenix to others.

As the saying goes, hiding your hardships in order not to worry others is the practice of a bodhisattva. To the people who have been battered by the rough and tumble of life, we who cultivate our minds shouldn't add any more to their suffering. We should always practice compassion, and always try to serve nectar from the sweet spring of life to those with much pain in their minds.

THE ZELKOVA TREE

A picnic crowd rests briefly under the zelkova tree in the park and then leaves. The neighboring town's children take over the vacated tree shade, cooling down the heat of their raucous play, and then leave for the mountain streams to splash in the water. As midday passes, a few of the town's elders gather under the tree to talk about the passing affairs of the world and then leave one by one as night approaches.

In the empty park where the sun has set, little mice make their appearance. After running around for the cookie crumbs that were spilled by the visitors, they look for their homes. As the night deepens, a full moon floating in the sky illustrates the evanescence of the world.

The shaded ground under the zelkova tree is a place of excitement and anticipation for the picnicking crowd searching for the mystery of nature, a playground mixed with joy and innocence for youths, a place of the sorrow of alienation and regrets about life for the town's elders, and a place of competition over food for the mice.

All the world's a stage, as Shakespeare once said. The actors, who play their parts and exit, are destined to pass this place again. Meanwhile, it must be the tree's habit to carefully record all the actors' stories, both happy and sad, in its two hundred growth rings.

The blue, porcelain sky abruptly enters my vision as I raise my eyes. The cool, blue sea spreads far away and thick forests mysteriously cut across the mountain tops. Even the wide open field—this beautiful land—must be a stage on which we stay briefly and eventually leave behind. The family that we love, the friends whom we love, the nation that we love—when their time is over, the cause and condition, the karmic ties, cease. Thus all will scatter to each of their paths like a flock of sparrows in the morning sky.

Who wrote this play in which we have to laugh, cry, and exit according to the script? No God can write it, nor can Buddha. Only your own mind can write it.

THE VIRTUE OF WATER

Water is the source of all life. Living one's life like the flow of water means practicing the truth, the Dharma.

If there is a rock, water does not fight to go through it but goes around it. If it goes under a rectangular bridge, it takes the shape of the bridge; if it goes through a round pipe, it takes a round shape. Neither does water cling to its color. Instead it washes all things to make them clean. For water does not have the stubbornness of "I," it is in the state of "no mind." When people listen to the murmuring of a stream, it puts them at ease.

People always try to put themselves higher, but the water always finds the lowest place. The stream lowers itself to become a river, and the river lowers itself even further until it cannot go any lower and reaches the sea.

Water does not compete to go ahead of others, and water knows how to wait for the right moment. People who cultivate their minds should live like flowing water and learn a great deal from it.

MY MIND TREE

A tree shakes when the wind blows, and it stands still after the wind passes. However, when the mind's tree hears a disturbing story, it stands still at first. Then, after the wind of disturbance passes, it shakes violently for days to come, thinking things like, "I should have said this," or "I should have said that."

What is the reason that the mind's tree shakes for many days after a single gust of wind? It is because it still has impurities. Unlike the mind's tree, all things in nature are calm after the wind passes.

Look at my mind's tree that violently shakes by itself in the moonlit night or on a bright sunny day. What would the stream that flows over there, or the rock next to it, or the birds in the sky, say?

KASHYAPA, WHAT IS THE MIND?

Once, the Buddha said to Kashyapa:

What mind is the mind that is tainted by sexual desire, that shakes in anger, or that is blinded by ignorance? Is it the mind of the past, the present, or the future? If it is the mind of the past, it has already disappeared; if it is the mind of the future, it has not come yet; and if it is the mind of the present, it no longer remains.

The mind is neither within, without, nor anywhere else. Because the mind has no form, it cannot be seen with the eyes, and it cannot be touched. The mind does not appear, it cannot be recognized, it cannot be named. No Tathagata has ever seen the mind. It cannot be seen now, and it probably will not be seen in the future. How does such a mind work?

Because the mind is like an illusion, it appears in many different forms from the deluded discriminations.

Because the mind is like the wind, it travels far and cannot be caught, and it does not show its form.

Because the mind is like the flowing river, it passes without stopping.

Because the mind is like the flame of a lamp, when it is lit by a cause, it lights up the environment.

Because the mind is like lightning, it does not even remain for a moment and it ceases in a split second.

Because the mind is like an empty space, it becomes dirty from unexpected smoke.

Because the mind is like a monkey, it cannot stay still even for a moment and it constantly moves around.

Because the mind is like an artist, it creates many different forms.

The mind does not stay in one place. It generates many doubts at once.

The mind goes alone; it is not merged with a second mind.

Because the mind is like a king, it rules everything.

Because the mind is like an enemy, it brings up all the suffering.

Because the mind is like a house built with sand, it thinks impermanent things are permanent.

Because the mind is like a gadfly, it thinks that what is dirty is clean.

Because the mind is like a dream, it believes that what is not mine is mine.

Because the mind is like an enemy, it always awaits and rejoices at weakness.

As the mind is moved by self-righteousness or shaken by anger, sometimes it becomes arrogant, and sometimes it becomes dishonorable.

Because the mind is like a thief, it steals all the good roots planted in the past.

The mind likes beautiful color, like a moth that flies

into a fire.

The mind likes sound, like the sound of the drum on the battlefield.

The mind likes the smell of decadence, just as a boar likes the smell of a rotten corpse.

The mind likes taste, like a dog that salivates when looking at food.

The mind likes the sensation of touch, like a fly stuck to an oily plate.

Even if you exhaustively observe the mind like this, the true nature of the mind cannot be known. It cannot be found. The thing that cannot be attained does not exist in the future, in the present, or in the past.

The thing that does not exist in the future, in the present, or in the past exists by transcending the future, the present, and the past.

The thing that exists by transcending the three time periods is neither existent nor nonexistent.

The thing that is neither existent nor nonexistent is never created.

The thing that is never created does not have self-nature.

The thing that has no self-nature does not arise.

The thing that does not arise never ceases.

The thing that never ceases never passes.

If it does not pass, there is neither going nor coming. There is neither dying nor being born.

The thing that has neither going, coming, dying,

nor being born has no creation of cause and effect.

The thing that has no creation of cause and effect has neither creation nor change. It is in the state of inaction. This is the innate nature of a saint.

Just as empty space is equal to wherever it is, that innate nature is equal in everyone. That innate nature has no discrimination [between different beings], because in the end every being is from one essence.

Because the innate nature that has departed from such discrimination of the body or the mind is peaceful, it follows the path to nirvana.

Because that innate nature cannot be defiled by any suffering, it is pure.

Because that innate nature has no attachment of "I am doing something," or the attachment of "mine," it is not mine.

The mind's true nature is neither truthful nor untruthful. Ultimately, it is balanced, because it is not biased toward anything.

That true nature is the most supreme truth. It transcends this world.

Because that true nature is not originally created, it can never cease.

Because that true nature always exists, it is eternal.

Because that true nature is the most supreme nirvana, it is happiness.

Because that true nature has been purified of all defilements, it is clear.

Because that true nature has no ego when you look

for it, it is egoless.

That true nature is absolutely pure. Therefore, one should quest for the wisdom within and not drift outside oneself. Even if someone is angry at you, do not be angry in return. Even if you are getting beaten upon, do not beat upon the other person in return. Even if you are being criticized, do not criticize others in return. Even if you are being mocked, do not mock the other. Then look into your mind and see exactly who the focus of anger is, who is being beaten up, who is being criticized, who is being mocked.

Spiritual seekers should thus collect their minds and should not be shaken in any situation.

From the Kashyapa chapter of the Heap of Jewels Sutra

N i n e

Enlightened Masters

BODHIDHARMA

Bodhidharma was a prince from southern India. After entering the Buddhist order, he taught students in India and also went to China to propagate the Dharma.

Once, on his way to China from India, he found an enormous serpent lying dead on a narrow path. In the area of Assam, there are serpents that feed on elephants, and this was one of them. When this serpent's carcass starts to rot, it attracts poisonous insects with its odor and blocks traffic for three years. Neither Bodhidharma nor anyone else would have been able to travel on that road, and to clear away the carcass would have required a couple of hundred people. Such a group of people was not available at the time.

Carefully looking at the dead serpent, Bodhidharma found that it hadn't been dead for too long, so he shed his own body and let his mind enter the serpent's carcass in order to drive it away. After moving the thing for seven days with much effort, he returned to the place where he had left his body, but it was nowhere to be found. Instead, there was the body of a bald-headed man with a ruffian's face. It so happened that when a Taoist ascetic meditating in the caves at Kun Lun Mountain saw the neat-looking body lying there on the ground, he shed his own body and walked away wearing the better looking one.

Bodhidharma had already opened a Zen monastery in China and, at that time, was in the process of teaching students. If he didn't put on the ascetic's ugly body, he would have to wait for twenty years before he grew into a body with which he could teach his students again. So, he entered the ascetic's body and took its form.

When he came to China, his students did not recognize him at all. After spending a couple of months with Bodhidharma, one of the students said that he did not look like Bodhidharma, but that the way he used his mind—the way he carried himself—was like Bodhidharma.

Bodhidharma finally told them what had happened and was acknowledged by his students. This is the reason why portraits of Bodhidharma look the way they do today.

Bodhidharma's Dharma power, which enabled him to take off and put on his body, is indeed extraordinary. People who have not shed the desires of their flesh spend their whole lives as slaves to their own bodies, running errands for their bodies, while their minds' weeds grow up three feet high. We should be able to subdue and rule our bodies so that we can serve Buddha. Only when we can subdue and control our bodies are we freed from the desires of the flesh.

TWO MASTERS IN MYOHYANG MOUNTAIN

At a small hermitage called Geumseondae on Myohyang Mountain, two monks, each just over sixty years old, were diligently practicing meditation. One day, one of the monks said that he wanted to go sightseeing in Seoul, so he took his knapsack and left for the city. After leaving the monastery, walking down in the direction of Anju and Bakcheon, he saw a butcher working in a meat shop. He saw the butcher separating the meat from the bone, cleaning out the meat that was deep inside the bone. He thought to himself, "We should thoroughly clean out the discriminations in our minds like that. I suppose a spiritual seeker should also try to be a butcher."

That very night, when his thought had progressed that far, he shed his body and passed on to the next life. Since his Dharma had been awakened, any decision arising in his mind was realized immediately.

After a while, the wife of the butcher gave birth to a child. The baby was bright, and his behavior surpassed the ordinary. The old monk had been born as the butcher's baby. Since he was born with his won to become a butcher, he was immersed in his work. Soon his family became wealthy from his diligence. In no time, he reached his nineteenth year.

Meanwhile, the monk who still resided on Myohyang Mountain was now over eighty years old, and he was nearing his time to change his body. For the first time, he searched with his mind's eye for his friend who had visited Seoul twenty years ago, and he saw him working as a butcher in the Bakcheon area. The old monk, in order to return to the mountain in a different body, first needed to leave the hermitage in the charge of his friend. He looked at the young butcher with his wisdom-eye to see if his friend could return by himself. It seemed impossible for the young butcher to come back to the hermitage on his own, so the old monk went to Bakcheon to bring back his friend.

When the old monk stood before the butcher's house and looked inside, he saw a well-built young man who looked about twenty years old, working hard. Even while the monk beat his wooden clacker, the young man did not look up but was intent on his work. After a while, the monk beat his wooden clacker again. The young butcher did not think that a venerable master would look for a man of such low birth as himself, and he pointed the knife at himself, to ask if the master was looking for him. The master nodded his head.

Suddenly, a question arose in the young butcher's mind: "What am I doing here?" And as soon as he thought to himself, "By what cause was I born in this household and doing this job? This is not the path I am supposed to follow," he took off his work apron and walked toward the monk.

Little children will follow their mothers home for dinner without any hesitation. As soon as the master nodded his head, saying, "Yes, I am looking for you," the young butcher forgot everything about his work. Determination arose in the young man's mind to follow the monk and return to his original path. I wonder if such determination came from the Dharma power of the master who wanted to take his friend back. Or perhaps, because the young butcher had been following the path toward Buddha for many of his past incarnations, he was suddenly awakened to his original path.

Just then, the young man's parents and siblings came out, having heard the sound of the wooden clacker. The young butcher looked at his family once. Then, without a word, he followed the monk who walked a couple of steps ahead of him. None of his family was able to stop him. The reason the butcher was born into that household was because he thought being a butcher might help his spiritual practice—not because he had any karmic tie to that household. Therefore, the moment he awakened a strong vow to renounce the world, no one could oppose his vow.

For many hours the master and the young man walked without saying a word to each other, not even "Where are you going?" or "Why are you following me?" Renouncing the secular life and seeking Buddha had been deeply ingrained in the young man for many lifetimes—it had almost become his habit. Soon, they were climbing past a hill and going up the valley. Even though it was the first time that the young man had been there, it seemed very familiar to him.

When they finally arrived at the monastery, everything seemed comforting to the young man. The temple grounds, the mortar, the kitchen, and everything else was what the young man had seen before. Since he was hungry, he made himself a meal and then fell into a deep sleep. As he woke up in the morning, the ringing of the bell and the beating of the wooden clacker sounded very pleasant. After three days, his mind became calm and quiet, and then he was awakened to the ability to see his past lives.

At that moment, the young man yelled roughly at the eighty-year-old man, "Why were you so late in bringing me here?" Becoming a butcher had been to help him cultivate his mind, whether it actually helped him or not. Buddhist monks usually renounce the worldly life to look for their teachers and monastery at around age thirteen, and since the young man had wasted seven extra years, he complained to his friend.

The eighty-year-old monk said with a smile, "I was so busy with my practice and with looking into my mind that I didn't have time to think about you."

What a perfect and truthful attitude toward the practice of cultivating his mind! We usually attach our minds to money, fame, and material possessions. But this master was so intent on his practice, he did not even have time to pay attention to his friend's affairs.

The nineteen-year-old man and the eighty-year-old man were talking casually like friends, for there was no doubt that they had been friends in the young man's past life. The young man was probably diligent in his practice from then on, and his friend must have received a new body in which to come back to Geumseondae.

MASTER HAKUIN

There was a Japanese Zen master named Hakuin who was revered as a living Buddha. The daughter of one of his followers became pregnant out of wedlock. Her father was furious and pressed hard to find out who the father was. "Whose bastard is it?" he asked her angrily.

Cornered, the daughter named an unthinkable person. "Master Hakuin," she answered. The father was baffled. Since it was the child of the master he revered, he could do nothing but forgive his daughter, and when later a boy was born, he took it to the master.

Whenever his followers or the townsfolk asked the master whether it really was his child, he always said, "Yes" with a smile. He gave love to the baby and raised him with great care. Consequently, his reputation was destroyed; some considered him a heretic rather than an enlightened master. His followers' visits also declined.

Master Hakuin, however, begged for alms, raised the baby with difficulty and gave not a single excuse. One day, the child's young parents came to see him. They bowed to him and shed tears of repentance, the mother saying, "Even though he is our child, I could not tell the truth to my father, for I felt that he would have killed me on the spot. I lied and told him that it was your baby. I saved my own life, but I have damaged your reputation severely. How can I ever be forgiven for my sin?" The master simply handed over the child to them and calmly smiled without saying a word.

Had we been in his situation, would we have been able to smile like him? His is a truly enviable mind-set. A person who is freed from the notion of self has no such thing as an "I," so there is nothing to be embarrassed about.

Looking at this story from a different point of view, one might recognize the role that notions imprinted in one's past incarnations play in creating such mishaps. Through such a notion, or because of a similar karmic hindrance in a past incarnation, one could experience misfortune in this lifetime. Therefore, when you are wronged and no one listens to you despite your explanations, just surrendering your arising mind (such as your hurt feelings) and calmly accepting the situation may be the wisest thing to do.

T e n

The Path That We All
Tread Together

THREE VEHICLES

There are three types of people who pursue spiritual practice: those who ride in the goat's vehicle, those who ride in the deer's vehicle, and those who ride in the white bull's vehicle.

Those who ride in the goat's vehicle follow the spiritual path because they do not like the sufferings of their bodies. They beg Buddha for their family's health, their economic well-being, and their happiness. These are the people who offer up one meal's worth of grocery money to Buddha and demand ten years' worth of living expenses.

Like merchants trying to make a profit, theirs is the mentality of doing business with Buddha. One must plant wealthy causes to be well off and plant happy causes to live happily. The people who ride in the goat's vehicle, however, only beg from Buddha and forego planting the causes. The goal of spiritual practice, however, is to change one's poor mind into a wealthy one—to condition one's miserable mind into a happy one—because everything is accomplished with the mind.

Those who ride in the deer's vehicle have more wisdom than the people who ride the goat's vehicle. These people know that this universe is built from the results of planted causes. They try to achieve bright results by diligently planting bright causes. They conduct their personal relationships in this way. They put much care into their children's education from the beginning, they invest plenty in their businesses, and they keep up their health early in their lives. And with thorough mental preparation, they live in readiness for every situation in their lives. These people live their lives brightly and successfully.

Thirdly, there are those who ride in the white bull's vehicle. These people know that what happens in their minds reflects what happens in the universe, outside their minds. Therefore, they accept the phenomena of the universe into their minds to enlighten those phenomena. Since these people's realization is one with the entire universe, it is the great vehicle and the most supreme vehicle.

They view sentient beings' problems as their own and resolve those problems to benefit many beings. With this type of enlightened person's won and capacity, wars and disasters can be prevented, and the people's minds can be calmed. Such is the path of the bodhisattvas, which lights up the realm of sentient beings. We should all ride in the white bull's vehicle to tread the path of the great vehicle.

WHEN ONE PURSUES THE PATH, NINE GENERATIONS BENEFIT

Just as radio stations send out radio waves, so the human mind sends out mind waves. The waves of the mind spread out in all directions of space. If a son who is far away in Seoul is sick or worried about something, his mother can sense such conditions through intuition or feel it through her dreams. This is the simultaneous transmission and reception of mind waves.

Similarly, one person's merit of opening his heart to the bright radiance—the merit of devoting himself to spiritual practice—is passed on to nine generations in all directions: to one's ancestors, one's grandfather, one's great grandfather, and so on, up nine generations; to one's descendants, one's grandchildren, one's great grandchildren, and so on, down nine generations; to one's relatives, uncles, cousins, and so on. One receives and feels directly all the mind waves that go back and forth in all directions. Karmic ties are linked in this way, both vertically and horizontally, and involve thousands of people.

If you lack spiritual cultivation and are quick to anger, are unstable, or greedy, or judgmental of others' faults, then you will send out your level of mind wave to the thousands of people within the boundary of your nine generations. People who have karmic ties with you will receive such mind waves and will suffer from them.

However, if you have cultivated your mind well enough to use it at a high level, then you will send out bright and healthy waves.

Thousands of people will feel joy through you. Also, if your practice is advanced enough so that you can receive others' dark mind waves and surrender them to Buddha, you will liberate their inner sufferings, wash away their dark shades, and illuminate their minds.

Moreover, the number nine implies infinity, as in the expressions "ninefold palace," "ninety thousand li of distant sky," or "nine thousand worlds." In Buddhism, "nine generations" means a countless number of ancestors and people who have karmic ties with you. Therefore, nine generations could mean all the beings in the universe. When Shakyamuni Buddha attained Buddhahood, many people became enlightened. The entire human race is receiving one Buddha's grace forever.

There is a saying, "If a monk is produced in a family, he illuminates the household." If he is someone who has awakened the Dharma power, his household and his hometown will receive the benefit. If an enlightened person is born, the entire nation will receive the benefit. If one person attains the ability to see one's past lives, thousands of people will attain the ability to perceive their past lives. When one person becomes enlightened, the whole universe is illuminated.

Buddhadharma—Buddhism—is more than just what occurs in physical reality. The inner radiance, knowingly and unknowingly, illuminates the whole spiritual realm.

ABOUT GIVING

Start with your mind to practice the mentality of giving

Very often, if people have worked their whole lives in public service or office jobs, they will pull out a cigarette only for themselves when they smoke. People who run businesses, however, frequently develop a giving mind regarding their cigarettes in order to close deals and get acquainted with clients. When the mind that has been conditioned for many years becomes firmly molded, actions follow naturally.

The giving mind is righteous and joyful. It is an alive mind. The begging mind, however, is a broken mind, a dead mind. Even with just a cup of coffee, the moment you decide to serve it to someone else, you feel secure and confident.

The giving mind cleanses that innate nature of pulling everything toward "me." Just as your arms bend toward you, people tend to pull every beneficial thing toward themselves. Such a trait is inevitable as long as people have egos.

When a poor relative or someone seeking charity visits us, we start putting up our guards first with our minds. It is the mind of not giving and of treating him or her coldheartedly. The mind is not material wealth. Even if we cannot provide him or her with the material wealth they seek, why can't we at least give with our minds? With material goods, you have to be in the right financial situation to be able to give, but mind is not the same way. If your mind is always that of giving, it directly becomes merit.

Give of your material possessions to accumulate great merit

If you give with the expectation of being rewarded, that is a business transaction and not an act of giving. For the person doing the giving, the receiver's joy should be sufficient reward. If one can give equally to strangers and to animals as one does with friends and family, one will accumulate merit.

When you lend money to someone, why not lend the money with the intention of just giving it away? If you did that, you would not be bound by the person who borrowed your money. If he paid you back, you would be as happy as if you had found free money. If the person did not pay you back, you would not suffer from it, and your mind would be free. However, if you lend with the expectation of being paid back, your mind will be concerned and anxious every time you experience financial difficulty. Such worries tie down your mind.

Donation of Dharma

Donation of Dharma means giving Buddha's teachings— such as the Diamond Sutra—to spread the method of cultivating one's mind or to share your experiences of spiritual practice with others.

The teacher gives his life to the student

The sun gives light to all life forms to help them grow. No

matter how many life forms receive the sunlight, there is always enough. Like the sun, the Buddha gives out life to all sentient beings. The moment we turn to Buddha, we receive the luminous energy of Dharmakaya and gain new strength. By reading the sutras and by reciting Buddha's names or mantras, we receive strength from the Buddha.

A teacher gives the entire energy of his life—energy gained through his spiritual practice—to his students. Since students take away energy, he has to recharge his energy through spiritual practice. If, by reciting *Mireukjon Yeoraebul*, you constantly surrender your thoughts to Buddha, your energy will be recharged and you will be able to give it out to those who need it.

Once, upon meeting a person who did not follow the spiritual path, my mind felt as if it were suffocating and in pain because I felt his painful mind. When your mind is calm, you can directly feel another's mind. While I was talking to him, a bright light suddenly came out of my chest and entered him. It left a big hole, and my body was depleted of all its strength. My mind felt smothered and uncomfortable, and my chest hurt as if it were burning. I had just witnessed the reality of how sentient beings take life energies from one another.

The bigger the luminosity a person enjoyed in his past life, the more advanced a practitioner he was, the more energy his mind tries to absorb in this life. If such a person does not cultivate his mind in this life, and his mind is full of karmic hindrances, his mind will try to absorb as much bright energy as he held in his former vessel. Therefore, when an advanced practitioner encounters such a nonpractitioner, it can be very painful for the practitioner. This is the same reason why sick people like healthy people, because the sick people receive the healthy energy. One has to practice surrendering continually to recharge one's energy.

Spiritual practitioners and enlightened masters give all their energies to their students. They give even their lives. To raise their students, they give without the discriminative notion of giving. Because such acts cannot be seen, ordinary people do not understand—the grace of one's teacher can only be understood at a high level of wisdom.

As it is written in the Dhammapada:

> Just as a spoon cannot know the taste of the broth, a foolish person cannot know the true Dharma, even after attending an enlightened person for a whole lifetime. But just as the tongue tastes the broth, so shall a wise person quickly know the true Dharma, even after spending only a brief time with an enlightened person.

GIVING WITHOUT SEEKING REWARD

Having a healthy mind means having the generosity to give what is ours to others, even though they may be fiercely attached to themselves and struggling with their lives. Our minds try to make everything ours, whether it is money, power, position, or someone else's mind. In trying to obtain these limited things, conflicts arise. The flame of conflict encourages even more "me," "mine," and "my victory."

In the mind that is freed from the "I," no attachment remains. That mind is an empty mind. Without the desire for others' possessions, the empty mind does not cause another person to put up his or her guard. The craving mind, however, is weighed down by such anxieties as "What if I cannot obtain it? What if I lose it?" because there is an attachment to the object that it seeks. In the healthy, giving mind, there may be some such worry as "What if the other person doesn't accept it?" but in the end, the giving mind is simply full of joy.

Once, when Master Baek was walking down a road with other spiritual practitioners, he saw a woman moaning in pain from drinking caustic soda. Seeing this, he told his students to take her back to the monastery and care for her. One of the bosallims carried her back to Anyang-am, nursed her, and provided her with medicine.

Since this woman was in hellish pain, she showed no gratitude from the beginning. She couldn't overcome the physical pain, screaming many days and nights without sleeping, nor could she eat anything properly, because her gullet had melted from drinking the caustic soda. Furthermore, she didn't want to take even the expensive foreign medicine that the bosallim had bought for her. Thus, every time the bosallim saw this woman, she began to think, "What am I doing with this total stranger here? Did I come here to serve Buddha or this hungry ghost?" and a feeling of reproach arose in the bosallim's mind.

Seeing how the bosallim felt, Master Baek said, "The healthy, giving mind does not quarrel over the right and wrong of the receiving person's weak and frail mind." When there is no ego, the giving mind asks nothing from the receiver. After one hundred days of devoted care and prayers, the woman was cured, and left the monastery with gratitude.

One day a year later, while attending Master Baek, the bosallim passed by the Chinese embassy along with some other practitioners. The sick woman, whose name was Boksuni, was standing by the road with a baby on her back, apparently now the servant of some household. The bosallim who had cared for Boksuni was glad to see her. She tried to go near her, calling out her name, but Boksuni ran away from her as if she were ashamed, either because of the incident that had happened the year before or of her current status. When the bosallim tried to follow her, Master Baek said, "Shouldn't you just be happy to see your successful mind—the result of your healthy, giving mind? Why did you try to follow that slab of flesh just then?"

He was saying that saving the woman's life had been the success of the bosallim's mind, for she planted merit through that virtuous act. So now, when she should have been grateful and satisfied with the results, why was she seeking recognition and credit for her deed? Once she heard this Dharma lecture, she was ashamed of being unmindful and of not surrendering at that instant and instead letting her mind leave her to follow that woman.

COMPASSION

We raised many cows at Sosa Monastery. Sometimes, they gave birth to stillborn calves. Whenever that happened, somehow the people from our town or the next town knew it right away and came to ask for the meat. Since our diet was purely vegetarian, and since the calf must have been born at our monastery due to a close karmic tie with us, we couldn't imagine eating the meat.

When we gave away the stillborn calf while wishing, "Feed those people with your flesh, and may you plant as much merit as you can," people took it gratefully. But sometimes no one would come to claim the meat. Usually people came within two hours of the birth to take the meat, but once in a while no one came even after a full day.

Our master said that if the calf had planted merit in its past incarnations, people would come to take the meat, and the calf would accumulate more merit. But if the calf had not planted any merit, people would not come, and there would be no one to help the calf plant any merit. He said that when a cow is killed in a slaughterhouse and becomes food for thousands of people, it plants the merit of feeding others with its own flesh. If it is reincarnated as a human, it becomes a wealthy person, earning between two hundred and one thousand sacks of rice a year. Master Baek meant that when you feed others with your own flesh, you accumulate great merit.

Once no one asked for the meat of a stillborn calf, and

eventually the meat went bad. When the master saw this, he told us to bury the carcass and plant a fruit tree over it. If you feed ripened fruit having used a calf as fertilizer to spiritual seekers, the calf gets to plant merit. However, it was during the summer, and I couldn't get a fruit tree, nor was there anyone around who knew about fruit trees, so I was at a loss. I had to plant a willow tree instead. After four years, the willow grew huge, fed by the nutrients of the calf's carcass.

That winter, we had other firewood, but I intentionally used the wood from the willow tree and heated the rooms of many spiritual seekers. As I was heating the rooms, I invoked a won to Buddha, "By the merit of keeping these spiritual seekers warm, may this calf meet enlightened masters, listen to their teachings, and awaken to their teachings in every future incarnation, so that he may serve and accumulate great merit before Buddha, barwon!" Until I had done that, it had been a burden on my mind, but when I used the firewood and made the won, I felt as if a weight had been lifted from my shoulders. I realized later that my master had given me the task to make me practice compassion.

After that incident, even when a monastery's cat died, we buried it with a thoughtful won. We always found something that might accumulate merit for the past owner of its body.

MASTER WONHYO AND THE RACCOON CUBS

During the Silla period, Master Dae An found some raccoon cubs that had lost their mother, and to save them he went to the town's public well to beg for some milk from the women. The women, deeply moved by the master's precious Dharma lecture, happily donated some milk.

Master Dae An carried the milk in a bowl and climbed over a steep hill until he finally reached the raccoon cave, where the young cubs were eagerly waiting for their food. Feeling pity for the cubs, he fed and raised them for many days with much compassion.

When the cubs had grown enough for their eyes to shine, Master Wonhyo came to visit him. Master Dae An asked Master Wonhyo to take care of the cubs for a few days, for he had some urgent business to attend to elsewhere.

Master Wonhyo raised them with great care, but two of them died. Wonhyo, who boasted that he was the foremost Buddhist master of Silla, could not face Dae An again. Master Wonhyo thought to himself that Master Dae An had been raising the cubs for fifteen days when they were still tiny forms of flesh and blood, but because of his own thick karmic hindrances and lack of wisdom, he had caused their death. He deeply repented and took this as an opportunity to awaken his devotion again.

When Master Dae An returned, he consoled Wonhyo, "There was no way you could have held on to those whose karmic ties were ceasing." A crow was cawing noisily in front of Wonhyo, who couldn't say anything. Then Master Dae An said, "Let's fill the crow's stomach and let the raccoons plant merit," and threw the dead raccoon cubs to the sky. The crow that was circling the area sensed his luck and snatched them away like lightning.

MEMORIAL DAY

Many soldiers sacrificed their lives on the battlefield protecting their country. Where are these many spirits now? What are they doing? As spirits, what form do they take? One cannot help but wonder about the afterworld.

It was reported that the North Korean army alone lost no fewer than two hundred thousand men at the Nakdong River during the Korean War. After the war, I heard stories from the locals who had settled by the riverside. They said that more than once terrifying screams had kept them awake at night, and that such sounds were heard by many. It is said that these sounds of wailing were at their most intense for three years, and later gradually subsided.

Once, around 10 o'clock at night, I saw a student standing by the stream running behind the Uhyeon Monastery. He was wearing a creased school uniform and a crumpled cap, and his head was bowed. He looked about eighteen years old. There is an area four hundred meters from the Uhyeon Monastery where, under the command of General Kim Seok-won, a student named Kim Chun-sik and forty-eight other young men fought valiantly and died, as they tried to stop the communist forces from entering the city of Pohang during the war. Unable to come to terms with their early deaths, they had now become spirits wandering in tears. I could sense their heartfelt yearning for deliverance.

In the same year, when I turned thirty-five, I had the task of enshrining Diamond Sutras across the country on Memorial Day.

I began a movement to read the Diamond Sutra at 10 o'clock in the morning on June 6th of every year to deliver the countless souls who had fought to defend their country and nation—going back to the time before Dangun (the first ruler of Korea), and from the founding of Korea by Dangun to Ancient Joseon under Emperor Chiwu, through to the dynasties of Goguryeo, Baekje, Silla, Gaya, Balhae, Goryeo, Joseon and so forth.

When I was residing at the Seoul Monastery, I used to visit the National Cemetery with the bosallims to read the Diamond Sutra. Once, a bosallim told me that her cousin, who was buried in the cemetery, appeared in her dream that night, and told her that he was extremely grateful for the reading of the Diamond Sutra earlier that day. Often spirits cannot depart from their place of death, and remain there owing to bitter resentment, an unfulfilled wish, or other reasons. However, before the Dharma power of the Diamond Sutra and the white radiance of *Mireukjon Yeoraebul*, all such resentment, pain and suffering is liberated.

May the souls of those who died defending their country, and the souls of those who are unable to move on, who remain lost as wanderers—may all spirits receive a human body, read the Diamond Sutra and surrender well by reciting *Mireukjon Yeoraebul*, so that they may serve Lord Buddha well.

THE MISTAKE OF TEACHING OTHERS

After Master Zhao Zhou's spiritual practice had matured, he traveled around China and taught many students.

Once he went to see his friend at a monastery in the Shan Dong area. His friend's twelve-year-old novice monk brought two and a half wheat cakes on a tray. Since Master Zhao Zhou was the guest, Master Zhao Zhou thought the young monk would serve him first, but the novice monk served a cake to his master first. Master Zhao Zhou thought that now the young monk would serve him the other one and that the young monk would take the half. But the young monk did not offer the cake to Master Zhao Zhou at all. Instead, he put the one-and-a-half rice cakes in front of himself and started eating.

Because Master Zhao Zhou liked to teach others, he said sarcastically to his friend, "My friend, you should teach that child well."

His friend answered, "I do not want to ruin him by trying to correct his wrongs."

At that moment, Master Zhao Zhou had a great awakening. He looked back at his past and thought to himself, "How many times have I taught people to go the wrong way." That novice monk accumulated merit by awakening a master.

If a teacher molds his or her students with the intention of making Buddha happy, it is a radiant deed. But if he or she says, "I am molding them" and "I am teaching them," then it is the ego that is doing the teaching. The students feel uncomfortable, and they inherit the ignorance of their teachers. At such times, if the negative karmic hindrances of the teacher and the students clash with one another, the act of teaching cannot be a virtuous act. How often people bind and agonize others in the name of teaching!

A Buddha, who is perfect, can see the past, present, and future of his student with his wisdom-eye, and therefore can wisely lead the student according to the life the student has led. If you are not able to do that, you could lead a student in the wrong direction forever, or your student might end up feeling hostile toward you.

When someone asks you a question, answer him or her sincerely, and when you are not asked, do not force your teaching upon others. If you really want to teach, teach them after shedding yourself of the ego to teach, and then others will not be burdened by learning from you. For if you teach others only with your ego's desire to teach, you will be annoyed when others do not accept your lessons. Where there is annoyance, there cannot be the work of Buddha. At such a time, you should realize your limitations as a teacher and surrender that annoyance.

SAVING BEINGS IS BUDDHA'S JOB, OUR JOB IS SERVING BUDDHA

Master Baek lectured that the Buddha had cleansed all the eighty-four thousand discriminations from his mind, but there was still one discriminating mind left in him—the desire to deliver sentient beings. Once a Buddha, or fully enlightened person, surrenders even that discriminating mind, he or she remains as the radiance of the Dharmakaya, no longer receiving a physical body. That state is called Tathagata, and in such a state there is no desire to do anything. There is only responding to sentient beings.

Because Buddha is freed from "I"—because he has no ego—even when he leads sentient beings to salvation according to his vow, he stays bright and pure like the lotus that blossoms in muddy water. But when one who is not freed from the ego tries to deliver sentient beings, it is more problematic.

If you meet people and help them in order to serve Buddha, you impress Buddha's radiance in your mind and not the karmic hindrances of those people. However, if you step forward and say, "I will help and save others," then, in your mind, you fully imprint the people whom you've helped. Therefore, in either this or the next incarnation, you could easily become like those people—you could end up in the same situation. If, after helping people in need, you find you have imprinted their miseries in your mind and have become miserable yourself, it would be difficult to call your deeds bodhisattva activity.

Likewise, if you think that you helped someone, then because you are still attached to your help, you are bound to the other person through seeking a reward. Furthermore, in order to claim your reward, you might be born into that person's household. On the other hand, if you help others with the reverence of serving Buddha, you are freed from the karma of giving help and receiving a reward.

If you say to yourself, "I am helping you," your ego's poisonous energy burdens the other person, and your ego of helping makes the other person feel uncomfortable and ashamed. Do it instead in order to make Buddha happy and to serve Buddha. There is no ego in such a mind, and this will not hurt the other person's feelings. Leading sentient beings to salvation is Buddha's job. Our job is serving Buddha.

THE ENLIGHTENED BEING WALKS
ONE STEP AHEAD OF THE ORDINARY BEING

We often force others to do things that we haven't tried ourselves. We make them do things that are unreasonable. If you force others to do things that you cannot do, you imprint that action in your mind. As a result, in the future you will be forced by others to do an impossible job. How burdensome and painful your mind will be when that happens!

Likewise, you should not force others to do tasks that you were able to do previously but cannot do now. If you make others do a difficult job that you cannot handle in your present situation, you imprint sorrow in your mind.

Teachers should not present their students with subjects that are too difficult. A person who teaches others should be just one step ahead of his or her students. You have to lead them closely to give them the hope of being able to follow you. Also, in order to avoid showing too much of a gap between you and your students, you must cleanse yourself of your ego. Lead others by letting them learn one thing and realize one thing. Have them listen to one Dharma lecture and also practice it. Walk just one step ahead of them. Then, just as a puppy follows a piece of fish, they will follow you one step at a time, learning and practicing to gain all sorts of benefits. An enlightened being walks one step ahead of an ordinary being.

THE CHILDREN
WHO PRACTICE SURRENDERING

Daewu, a first grader in elementary school, had always heard his mother reading the sutra and had also heard Dharma lectures. He knew something about the practice of surrendering.

Because he was class president, he often had to go to the teachers' office. There were many teachers of whom he was afraid, and he felt timid, and sometimes, out of nervousness, he couldn't even speak to them. Sometimes he couldn't control his flustered mind—his face would turn completely red, and he would stutter, making little sense with his words. It was his job, however, and he couldn't avoid going, so it was always a problem for him.

One day, before he opened the door, he stopped himself because his heart was beating too fast. He turned aside and recited *Mireukjon Yeoraebul* for about two minutes. Then his mind was calm, and he was able to go inside the office to take care of his business.

Chorong, a third grader, once spent two hours in the evening doing her homework. The next morning, when she was getting ready to go to school, she found that her five-year-old brother had scribbled all over her notebook with a yellow crayon. Chorong became so angry that she was about to hit him with her fist, when suddenly she remembered the Dharma lecture that said to surrender by reciting *Mireukjon Yeoraebul*. She also remembered her mother saying that the child who surrenders well is the nicest child. She began to surrender with tears in her eyes.

Although they are only children, they are already putting the cultivation of their mind into practice. It is said that one who rules one's body is a sage and that one who rules one's mind is a saint. If we educate our children to rule their own minds, how bright and prosperous the future of this country will be!

E l e v e n

Reading the Diamond Sutra,
Surrendering the Mind

THE DIAMOND SUTRA,
SHAKYAMUNI BUDDHA'S
SPIRITUAL HOUSEKEEPING

Shakyamuni Buddha did not teach the Diamond Sutra to spiritual seekers at first, for it was too hard. Only after he had taught his students for forty years, when their practices had matured and the religious order was stable, did he teach the Diamond Sutra. Master Baek said that among the six hundred wisdom lectures the Diamond Sutra is the one that the Buddha wanted to teach the most.

My master tried many different methods and became confident with the Diamond Sutra and the practice of surrendering. Even in the Zen sects that preach not using language to transmit the teaching, the Diamond Sutra is accepted as the main sutra and is read universally.

The Diamond Sutra is the answer to the Venerable Subhuti's question, "If a good man or a good woman is determined to awaken the supreme enlightenment, how should he or she control and exert the mind?" Chapters 3, 4, and 5 directly answer Subhuti's question. In chapter 3, Buddha tells us to control our minds by turning all our useless thoughts, which cause us to be born as nine different sentient beings, into Buddhas: "All sentient beings will be led to nirvana." How then does one make Buddhas out of one's discriminating minds?

Being angry and practicing the vengeful mind conditions you to receive the body of a venomous snake. By clinging to material goods, sexual desires, and fame, you practice the mind of a serpent. According to how you condition the mind, a body is formed from among the nine categories of sentient beings, and you then receive that body. It means that when you surrender to Buddha whatever thought that arises, its delusion vanishes. In other words, we should surrender all thoughts, whatever they may be, until the mind is completely empty, by reciting *Mireukjon Yeoraebul* to the thought.

In chapter 4, Buddha says to practice giving without regard to appearances of sight, sound, smell, touch, flavor, or any other quality. How do we practice the mind-set of giving without regard to appearances?

As long as one has an ego, one cannot detach oneself from appearances. On the other hand, if one purifies the ego, everything one does will be detached from appearances. In order to purify your ego, whatever you do in your life, do it for Buddha. Instead of doing things for yourself, practice doing everything for Buddha. Make serving the Buddha the purpose of your life. By cleansing your ego this way, when your mentality of serving Buddha is mature, you can practice charity without regard to appearances. When you exert your mind in this way, free of attachment, your merit will be boundless, as incalculable as empty space.

In chapter 5, Buddha tells us to recognize that all of our ideas at our level are incorrect (for we still have an ego). He says that when we surrender all our inner discriminations to Buddha and see the universe with an empty mind, we will perceive the bright radiance of the universe, the Tathagata.

As you practice chapters 3, 4, and 5, gradually you will

become proficient in the state of exerting your mind without attachment.

Diamond is the hardest of all minerals. Unchanging wisdom that does not break can be called diamond *prajna*. With this diamond *prajna*, the teaching that leads us from the shore of samsara to the shore of nirvana is the Prajnaparamita Diamond Sutra. After teaching many people for forty years, the Buddha named this teaching the Diamond Sutra, for he was confident that everyone could be enlightened with this method.

WHY ONE READS THE DIAMOND SUTRA

When we read Shakespeare's *Hamlet*, we transcend both time and space, and become one with the spirit of Shakespeare four hundred years ago in Stratford-upon-Avon. We see the fields, streams, mountains, and oceans that continuously spring from his masterfully crafted words and imagery, and absorb the essence that permeates every corner of his writing.

Goethe put all of his philosophy, art, and experience of life into his great play *Faust*; he poured his whole mind into its words. *Faust*, therefore, is a part of Goethe's mind. To read this work is to join our own mind with that of Goethe. When we read his words, our spirit is united with his, and we travel to the Germany of two hundred years ago.

When we read the Diamond Sutra, which is the Buddha's enlightened mind and radiance, we travel beyond time and space to three thousand years ago to Jeta Grove in India. We communicate with Buddha, whose mind and body were in their healthiest state. Since we open our hearts to Buddha's radiance by reading the sutra, karmic hindrances that have frozen solid in the corner of our minds melt away, just as ice melts under the hot rays of the sun, and wisdom arises within us.

Just as fungi in inaccessible places are cleansed by sunlight, cleansing and gradually illuminating one's mind with Buddha's radiance is the purpose of reading the Diamond Sutra. It is very hard to read the sutra at first because we have been practicing the dark mind for countless eons, and we shy away when we suddenly face its brightness.

Reading the Diamond Sutra itself is cultivating one's mind. To cultivate one's mind is to become similar to Tathagata Shakyamuni. This means reading the sutra over and over to emulate Shakyamuni Buddha's wisdom, character, and compassion and to plant merit just as the Buddha did.

When we read the Diamond Sutra, we eradicate the dark shadows of our minds, the shadows that cause misfortune, and we free ourselves from worries. If you diligently cleanse all of your bitter mind, your boggled mind, and your self-defeating mind, the difficulties in your life will be resolved, and your wishes will be realized. You will become aware of the true nature of things, as your mind becomes clear and bright. Reading the Diamond Sutra is a way to practice reverence and serve Buddha.

HOW TO READ THE DIAMOND SUTRA

Master Baek said that when we read the Diamond Sutra, we should have the following attitude:

First, do not doubt that Shakyamuni Buddha, who was healthy both in his mind and his body, taught it to his students.

Second, believe that you are among his 1,250 students, listening to his words directly and trying to understand them.

Third, try to practice the things that you do understand.

Since it becomes overwhelming if you set your practice periods too long, practice for about one hundred days at first.

The method of studying the Eastern classics containing the words of saints and sages is different from studying Western books. Even if you do not know anything about these Eastern scriptures, just try reading them aloud at first. If you do this until you and the author become one, you will merge into his or her world.

This works for the Diamond Sutra as well. You should read it aloud over and over with reverence, as if you were sitting in front of Buddha listening to his lecture, until you become one with Shakyamuni Buddha. You should read it with the sound coming from your lower abdomen, one inch below the navel, in the lotus position or kneeling while keeping the hips and back straight.

TEN YEARS OF PRACTICE
AND NAMO AMITABHA BUDDHA

According to the scriptures, we have to journey for ten trillion and eight thousand li to find the Western Pure Land, where Amitabha Buddha resides. The sixth patriarch, Master Hui Neng, explained this statement: "Ten trillion refers to the ten evils, which are karmic hindrances in our minds, and eight thousand li refers to the eight evil ways opposite to the eight perfections. Thus journeying for ten trillion and eight thousand li means we have to eradicate the ten evils and eight errors." At such a time, we become Amitabha Buddha.

There is a saying, "Ten years of practice becomes Namo Amitabha Buddha." Once, a spiritual practitioner was practicing hard for ten years to meet Amitabha Buddha. After he was awakened, he found that he himself was Amitabha Buddha. This means that if we clear the ten evils and eight wicked ways we are Amitabha Buddha.

Master Naong left these verses:

Where is Amitabha Buddha?
No matter how much I look,
There is no way to find him outside the mind.
By surrendering all the discriminations of the mind,
One attains liberation to empty the mind.
Then the mind illuminates,

Exuding purple radiance from the body.

Last year, the grand master of Songgwangsa temple was quoted in a Buddhist newspaper. He said that, according to the scriptures, the period when Tathagata Maitreya will appear is due in five billion and sixty-seven hundred million years. This means that if one purifies and overcomes the five gates of sensation, six gates of desire, and seven gates of consciousness, one can become Tathagata Maitreya.

TATHAGATA MAITREYA,
WHERE SHAKYAMUNI BUDDHA'S MIND IS

Master Baek once lectured about an incident that occurred three thousand years ago at Vulture Peak in India.

Having cultivated their minds well, five hundred of Shakyamuni Buddha's students were sitting in peaceful meditation, in a state of samadhi, free of the three poisons—greed, anger, and arrogance. The Buddha walked toward them, radiating bright luminosity. The moment they saw the Buddha approach them, the Buddha's radiance was brilliantly reflected in the mirror of five hundred empty minds. The scene was incredibly magnificent and beautiful.

Buddha spoke with much joy: "You are all bright and full of radiance! By purifying the mind like this, you will ultimately attain Buddhahood."

But as soon as they heard Buddha's words, all of their illumination ceased at once and became dark again. They had thought to themselves,

"Good! Since I am radiant, I will surely attain Buddhahood by cultivating the mind," and for a split second they directed their attention to "I." Their egos had risen to darken them again.

However, while everyone else had become dark, there was one person who was shining even more brightly than before, and sharing his radiance with his surroundings. When Buddha looked into this person's mind, he saw one of even more reverence and gratitude. The person was thinking, "Lord Buddha, if it were not for you, how would I ever have heard such a precious teaching about how to become enlightened through cultivating the mind?"

Then, Shakyamuni Buddha gave a confirmation to him, saying, "You will achieve Buddhahood, succeeding me. When that happens, you will be called Tathagata Maitreya." The one who received the confirmation asked Shakyamuni Buddha, "World-honored one, why do you merely radiate your luminosity and not give it to sentient beings? I beg you to give your radiance to everyone."

Having heard this, Shakyamuni Buddha praised him greatly, saying, "The Dharma that you expound will indeed be greater and greater!"

The one who received the confirmation was Ajita, a prince of Andaman. The country of Andaman is an island nation located between India and the Malay Peninsula. To meet the Buddha, he crossed an ocean, sailed up the Ganges, and participated in the gathering at Vulture Peak. Before he started out, he had cut down a tropical bamboo tree much bigger than a man and used it as a boat to sail there.

The moment that Prince Ajita received the confirmation, he thought to himself, "How can I succeed to Buddha's lineage?" It took him twelve incarnations to cleanse that one discrimination that had arisen from such a heavy sense of responsibility. While cultivating his mind for twelve incarnations, it is said that he came to this world as many different saints.

Shakyamuni Buddha praised Gwanse-eum Bosal (Bodhisattva Avalokiteshvara), saying that we would fulfill our wishes by reciting *Namu Gwanse-eum Bosal*. For this reason, even though Shakyamuni Buddha is the basis of all, we forget about the Buddha. Instead, we attach our minds to the wish-fulfilling power of Gwanse-eum and claim that reciting *Namu Gwanse-eum Bosal* is the best practice.

Bodhisattvas are the ten different representations of the Tathagata. Since we must direct our minds to Buddha, who is at the root of those representations, to become more enlightened, we have to find where Shakyamuni Buddha's mind has gone. Shakyamuni Buddha's mind has gone to the radiant place of *Mireukjon Yeoraebul*—Tathagata Maitreya.

Reciting *Mireukjon Yeoraebul* is the path to serve the principal Buddha, Tathagata Maitreya, who succeeded the spirit of Shakyamuni Buddha. One Buddha's period of delivering sentient beings is said to be three thousand years. At first a red lotus blossoms; after a thousand years, the white lotus blossoms; after two thousand years, the yellow lotus blossoms; and after three thousand years, it is said to become a blue lotus. When the blue lotus blossoms, a Buddha will appear in the world. There are supposedly lotus flowers that are nearing three thousand years old, alive since the time of Shakyamuni Buddha.

When I was a student, we used to calculate the Buddhist era to be around 2,990 years long. Back then, there was about a five-hundred-year difference between the northern Buddhist era and the southern Buddhist era. But at the World Buddhist Conference, led by Japan and southern Buddhist countries such as Thailand, they determined the Buddhist era to be about twenty-five hundred years long. Since then, we have been using this dating system. But we can be sure that three thousand years have passed since the period of Shakyamuni Buddha by examining Master Hyecho's travel record in Ceylon.

In the Sutra of Maitreya's Rebirth Above, Maitreya's Rebirth Below, and Maitreya's Attainment of Buddhahood, Shakyamuni Buddha describes the world in which Maitreya Buddha will appear. He says,

> At that time, the night will become as bright as the day [today we can play sports under bright electric lights]. Towns will be connected closely enough for a rooster to fly between them [such as apartments, and crowded city buildings], and glass will be paved on the roads [asphalt]. When we go to the bathroom, the ground will break open to clear away the excrement [modern bathrooms]. Bad fruits will be replaced by good and delicious ones. People will be richly clothed and life will be comfortable. Sexual relationships between men and women will have become promiscuous.

According to the scriptures, this is the period when the next Buddha will appear. May all sentient beings plant merit as bright as daylight to serve the coming Buddha well, barwon!

Twelve

Stories of Cause and Effect

THE MASTER WHO WAS BORN AS A WATER BUFFALO

In southern China, there was an enlightened master who had 1,250 students. It would have been good if all of his students were diligent in their practices and in their daily chores. However, some were lazy and they neither devoted themselves to spiritual practice nor planted merit. The master always thought to himself, "How wonderful it would be if only my students would work as hard as the water buffalo we have here at the monastery."

They raised the gray water buffalo to cultivate and till the soil and the rice paddies. Every time the master saw the water buffalo working hard, he thought very fondly of it and photographed the buffalo's image in his mind. Just as an image is impressed on film when you press the camera's shutter button, so the workings of the mind also deeply record both good and bad things. Even though he was advanced in his spiritual practice, the master did not surrender his fondness for the buffalo well.

Much later, it was time for the master to pass on to his next life. As the master was sitting in the lotus position, one of his students asked him,

"Master, where will you be going?"

As the master watched himself, the buffalo was ripe in his mind, and he saw that he would receive the buffalo's body. It was a baffling, shocking revelation for him. "How could such an accomplished master as myself receive a cow's body?" But it was too late.

Even at that moment, had he surrendered that ripened mind of the water buffalo to Buddha, he could have liberated himself from it since his own mind had created the image. But he did not recognize this, and he answered his student without surrendering.

"I will receive the body of a water buffalo."

Thus, he had already made the decision. He did not know until then that he had photographed the water buffalo in his mind. Now that he had realized it, he could have surrendered that hardened impression. But an incident that you confirm is hard to revoke. Furthermore, spewing out the decision that is made within your mind is like declaring it to yourself and to the universe. Such an act is the reconfirmation and acceptance of the result.

Beings act like their previous incarnations for the first three years of their new lives. Although he was born as a water buffalo, when he saw his students, he often chased after them to teach them because they were neither diligent in their practice nor in doing their work. Unfortunately, all that came out of his mouth was "Moo." The students, not realizing that it was their teacher, thought the buffalo was trying to hurt them, so they tied it to a pole. How frustrated and outraged he must have been!

One moonlit night, tied to a pole as a water buffalo, he was lamenting his miserable lot when Shakyamuni Buddha appeared with the bodhisattvas. Coming upon the master tethered there, the Buddha helped the master shed the buffalo's body.

Just as where the sun shines brighter, the shadow is darker, so too, the more you generate the causal mind—such as a buffalo's mind—in a radiant monastery, the more quickly you prepare your future body for a lower realm of birth.

When I was studying under Master Baek, our monastery was a radiant place. When I generated a causal mind at Sosa, my body would become unusually heavy and uncontrollable, and I would just be dragging it around. My mind was not bright. After being scolded by my teacher for being absentminded, I would intensely surrender such a causal mind. Sometimes surrendering it diligently for an hour was enough to free me from that future birth in a lower realm. After surrendering such a cause, my mind was refreshed, full of reverence, and my body felt light. If you don't surrender the animal body you are supposed to receive in the future, you will become like that master in China.

You imprint both extremely good and extremely bad things on your mind. If, however, there is no cause in your mind to perceive something as good or bad, your mind will be in a state of nondiscrimination. Therefore, you will not be strongly drawn to animals, and you will not generate the causal mind for an animal rebirth. Thus you should surrender every arising thought, good or bad.

KING CHEOLJONG AND PAK YEONG -HO

Long ago, a wealthy man on his way from Seoul to a prayer retreat at Mount Odae saw a monk writing on a piece of fallen leaf. The man from Seoul asked the monk why he was writing on a piece of leaf, and the monk said that it was because he did not have any paper. So the man from Seoul promised that he would bring him a roll of paper when he returned to Odae the following spring.

In the old days, paper was valuable. Because copying sutras and practicing meditation were the only joys he had, the monk's mind was directed to the wealthy man from Seoul, always wondering, "When will he bring the paper?" The next year, the monk asked someone who came to a prayer retreat at Mount Odae about the wealthy man from Seoul. He said that the wealthy man was building a temple at Odae.

By the merit of building the temple at Odae Mountain, the rich man from Seoul became King Cheoljong in his next incarnation. By the karmic cause of directing his mind to the rich man—always thinking, "When will he bring the paper?"—the monk became King Cheoljong's son-in-law, Pak Yeong-hyo.

Pak Yeong-hyo always wore silk, since he was a king's son-in-law, but he always used gray lining for his clothing. Because he had been a Buddhist monk and worn gray robes for many lifetimes, he had to wear gray-colored clothing at least under his outfit to feel comfortable.

Just as the Sutra of Causality tells us in detail, one plants great merit by building a temple. One temple is the basis for liberating many sentient beings' ignorance, karmic hindrances, and negative karmic ties. It is a place where they deepen their good roots. Because temples allow for the creation of positive karmic causes with the Buddha and provide the opportunity to practice the Dharma, building a temple, as in the case of King Cheoljong, creates exceedingly great merit.

As in the case of Pak Yeong-hyo, one is born near the person to whom the mind is directed during one's lifetime, for the mind is directed toward him or her again, even after the body is changed. By planting this cause in the mind, one becomes husband, wife, family, or friends.

WHEN A WICKED PERSON IS WELL OFF

People say that good people frequently lead miserable lives, and the wicked lead fortunate lives. They blame heaven for being indifferent. However, causes for such situations have been planted in past incarnations.

A man lives his whole life with virtue and a clear conscience, harming no one. When it is his time to die, he laments. He is full of regrets, thinking that helping other people, volunteering for the town, and doing all the things that others did not want to do was just a burden for him and his family. As he is dying, he thinks, "Even if I have to cheat others or harm others, I have to be well off first! That's the most important thing in life!" And as he dies, lamenting his poverty, he imprints that last thought in his mind. When he is born into his next incarnation, he lives his whole life trying to be wealthy, without worrying about compassion or morality.

As a person dies, the single notion that he focuses on becomes the foundation of his next life's mind. Since this man planted merit by doing good deeds in his past life, and since all the people who were indebted to him will pay him back in this life, he becomes wealthy. However, unless he cleanses his mind of that last determination, he will bear that selfish intention throughout his whole life. People who do not know the whole story will say that only a wicked person can be wealthy.

On the other hand, there is a person who cares only for his

wealth. He has no regard for morality or kindness. For his own gain, he even ignores his family. Such a person always realizes his mistakes at his last moment and sheds tears of repentance. Perhaps this is an innate morality or wisdom uniquely possessed by human beings. He regrets, "I have voraciously hoarded my wealth for my whole life, yet when I die I cannot take it with me." And he repents, thinking "The most important thing in life is to be a good, kind person first."

Because he dies with this last thought of goodness in his mind, when he is reincarnated, he lives his whole life with good intentions. However, since he did not do any good deeds for others or plant merit in his past life, he is always poor. He will live his whole life being harassed by the people that he harmed in his past life.

KARMIC RETRIBUTION FOR TAKING A LIFE

In China, they have a long scythe called a *jangnat*. Every time you swing it, you can cut an armful of grass. One summer day, a monk was cutting thick foliage and grass with such a scythe. On hearing the noise, a viper lifted up its head and was instantly decapitated. The monk felt a chill go down his spine, but it was too late. He recited Buddha's name and invoked prayers for the dead snake.

It is said that an animal that is killed by a human can easily receive a human body. Because the animal imprints the person who killed it at the last moment, it is reborn in the form of a human.

Twenty years later, the monk felt one day that his mind was unusually disturbed, so he meditated on it. He found that someone was coming to reclaim a debt. The viper that had died twenty years ago was coming to exact his revenge. A nineteen-year-old man then came to ask the monk to be his teacher. The monk wanted to refuse, but he agreed so that he could clear the karmic debt in that life.

Since they had only one room, they slept next to each other. The monk found out that for some time the young man had been sleeping with a knife at his waist, and that his eyes were becoming bloodshot. The young man was changing without even realizing it.

The monk made a dummy out of straw and hid it. Every time the young man went to sleep, the monk laid the straw dummy where he was supposed to sleep, next to the young man, and covered it with a blanket. The monk then continued his meditation at the other end of the room.

A few days after he had begun putting out the dummy, the young man suddenly woke up with his eyes half opened, still intoxicated with sleep. He felt for the blanket next to him, pulled out the knife and stabbed the dummy, then fell back to sleep. The monk was astonished.

All exchanges of karmic revenge between sentient beings transcend the bounds of morality and ethics. They paralyze human consciousness. When the young man woke up the next morning, upon seeing the master the poison instantly disappeared from his bloodshot eyes.

Karma that has been intentionally accumulated will cause an intentional karmic retribution, and the karma that has been unintentionally accumulated will cause an unintentional karmic retribution. Death and injury in auto accidents are not coincidental or random, but they are the result of causes planted in the past. If you can live without killing anything, your future will not be painful.

People do not know that when they kill an animal, the vengeance of the animal follows them around. Since it causes misfortune, it is best not to buy meat that was killed specifically for you, or meat from an animal that you heard or watched being killed.

Even when you are sick, you should use medicine that does not involve killing an animal for medicinal purposes. The animals that are supposed to become medicine are usually just receiving karmic retribution from their past lives. When it is time to exchange karmic debts with another, they might get killed like this—in the name of medicine. Another sign that it is time for you to exchange karmic debts is an unusual craving for meat.

After living in Europe for eleven years, my sister brought back a high quality leather jacket for me to show her gratitude. She felt that she was able to live happily in Europe because I supported her education. It was the first gift I received from her.

When Master Baek looked at the jacket, he said that the vengeance of the cow was attached to it. He also said that since the vengeance of the cow is often attached to leather, leather products are not acceptable. So I said, "What if I sell this jacket, and print Diamond Sutras with the money to plant merit for the owner of this leather, the cow?" And he said, "Don't start any karmic tie with the cow. Just give it back to your sister so they can resolve it between themselves." I followed his instructions. To enlighten one person, he paid careful attention to everything that might become a harmful obstruction.

I used to have a sheepskin jacket, and Master Baek told me it also carried the vengeance of the animal. He said that when the original owner of the sheepskin jacket—the animal—receives a human body and sees the jacket, it will cause misfortune between him and the new owner. Since then, I have avoided leather products.

WHY WE CANNOT
BUT SURRENDER THE MIND

When I had just entered Sosa Monastery, there was a person there who knew a lot about running the farm. He was very skinny and had a short temper. Once my master said to me, "Look at him. His snake's body has ripened, and it's shaking its head." With my master's wisdom-eye, such an image was directly reflected on his eyes, and when I looked at the man, it was just as my master said. I was so shocked that I thought my heart had stopped—he looked exactly like a snake shaking its head! I was troubled for the next few days. When I thought that anyone, including myself, could become like him through generating anger, I was worried sick.

I knew I had to pursue the spiritual path, but following it was difficult. Had I been ignorant, on the other hand, and not known that such a cause could create such a result, I could have lived my life without being burdened by it. I wondered why I had enough wisdom to know such a thing and to suffer from it.

Since it has conditioned a poisonous and vengeful mind, the snake holds its head erect and does not run away; rather, it chases after you out of spite. Out of fear, I fiercely surrendered any anger that arose in me as if my life depended on it.

ABOUT THE REPEATED CYCLE
OF BIRTH AND DEATH

All sentient beings can be divided into nine categories. Depending on how each group of sentient beings uses their minds, they are born in different forms and caught up in the fate of repeated birth. One's mind changes the style of one's life and one's environment.

Concerning those born from wombs, eggs, moisture, or by transformation

Let us look at four of the nine types of beings—those born from wombs, from eggs, from moisture, or by transformation:

Those born from wombs: If a being practices a dependent mind, it is born from a womb. For nine months, it depends on its mother's umbilical cord for its survival. After it emerges from the womb, it depends on its mother's nipple for about three years and is protected by the mother. Examples are mammals such as humans, dogs, cattle, and so on.

Those born from eggs: If a being practices an ungrateful mind, it receives the karmic result of being born from an egg. After receiving the nourishment from within its mother's body, it lives independently without regard for its mother. Examples are birds, chickens, ducks, and so on.

Those born from water: If a being practices a hiding mind, it receives a fish's body. Due to practicing a hiding mind while living on land, it can only live under water.

Those born by transformation: If a being practices a boasting mind when it is not qualified to do so, it receives a body born by transformation. For example, a fly is born from the transformation of a larva, and a mosquito is born from the transformation of a wiggler.

The case of different sentient beings

A dog's mind is that of scolding. A dog always barks—no other animal barks so noisily. Because a dog is made of a scolding mind, it barks with a scolding mind. The dog's mind is fit for a dog's body and not for a human body. When ninety-nine percent of your mind is ripe with a scolding mind, it completely becomes that of a dog and separates from the human body. Such separation of mind and body is called death.

A horse's mind is that of trying to get ahead of others. Because its wish is to win, it tries to outrun others, both on the race track and the battlefield.

A serpent's mind is one that tries to grasp a lot with a small body. Since the small body tries to grasp so much, it becomes long. The object it grasps could be money, fame, a man, a woman, and so on. In the old tales, there are stories about a big serpent protecting treasures in its coil. Such a thing is said actually to occur in real life. It must result from the owner of the treasure constantly practicing attachment to it.

A venomous snake's mind is an angry mind. Since a snake is always angry, its body is swollen with poison.

A rat's mind is that of a thief. It is the mind that always

looks for dark places and holes. It is neither confident nor righteous.

A cow's mind is that of being content with one's accomplishments. It is an ignorant mind that does not know what is going to happen in the future. Since it is satisfied with itself, its steps are always slow, and it is never in a hurry.

A fox's mind is a doubting and an unbelieving mind.

A fish's mind is a hiding mind. It hides under the sea.

A pig's mind is one of being greedy for food.

And there are many other examples. Whether human or animal, a being receives a body according to how its mind is conditioned.

According to one notion

Land animals feel that their lives are always threatened. In order to avoid being eaten, they do their best to be alert and on guard. The reason why the urine of rabbits and deer smells so bad is because of their nervousness. Similarly, a cow always instinctively looks into the distance to protect itself. Since they are so nervous all the time, hiding almost becomes their wish. When that wish deepens, according to the mental cause planted in the mind, the animal becomes a fish, for the hiding mind is that of a fish.

Once it lives under water, it feels confined. It wants to fly in the open. That mind causes it to become a bird in its next life. It always thinks flying would be wonderful, but now that it has flown, it feels empty; it misses a warm, cozy place. So it becomes a fish again, and if it feels cramped again, it can be born on land.

All sentient beings receive their bodies according to the single mind they generate. Whether you receive an animal's body through practicing the animal's mind, through imprinting the animal in your mind, through the won you have invoked, or because you have a karmic debt to a certain household, it all happens within a single mind.

As the scripture says, receiving a human body is as hard as dropping a needle from the sky to hit a mustard seed. If you were a child yesterday and you are forty already, the day after tomorrow you will be eighty. How much longer will you cling to your desires of flesh, money, and fame? How long will you be driven by these desires from here to there, letting time fly by, neither cultivating your mind nor practicing reverence to Buddha? Until you are at the doorstep of death? Because we can only devote ourselves to the spiritual practice when we have received human bodies, each moment we are alive is precious beyond compare.

A wayfarer who is journeying to a distant place stops and rests in an empty house. He cleans the house thoroughly. He dries the mildewed things in the storage room and the rice that has become moldy under the shade. He washes and dries the sweat-soaked clothes. He waters the withered garden and the vegetables to give them new life. He cleans the dirty well until its water is clear. He fixes the fallen door papers, and repairs the damaged walls. He lives in harmony with his neighbors, and he concentrates on study, knowledge, and the cultivation of wisdom.

Then, early one morning, he goes on his way. The next house he chances upon has plenty of food in storage, the vegetables are fresh in the garden, and the flowers in the flower bed are pretty, too. The walls are well built, all the clothes are clean, and a fresh stream flows by. His wisdom will be bright, his knowledge abundant, and he will be on good terms with his neighbors.

But at another empty house, another wayfarer, who is lazy, does not pick up the rice that has fallen on the floor. He lets the rats run around. He neither washes the smelly clothing nor fixes the broken doors and walls. He does not water the vegetables or flowers. Because he is heartless, he fights with others. He does not accumulate any knowledge or illuminate any wisdom. He just takes naps, and early one morning, he goes on his way.

The house he reaches after a long walk is so old that the walls have fallen. There is no rice, and the well is putrid. There aren't enough clothes, and the house is full of dust and garbage. The neighbors are all rough, and they fight constantly. He has no knowledge and no wisdom. He does not know how to do anything.

Everyone in the world receives the result of the causes they have planted. This is the life of repeated birth and death, samsara.

THE SOUND OF LAUGHTER

A wedding ceremony was held at a temple. During the solemn moment when the bride entered the Buddha hall, two guests in the crowd broke into laughter. It was Han Shan and Shi De. As if infected by the laughter, the guests, without even knowing why, started to chuckle. No one could hold it in. Eventually, they all broke into a roar of laughter, and the whole place became filled with people laughing out loud.

This was a once in a lifetime, all-important event for those who were holding the wedding. But since they were the hosts, they carried on with the ceremony, restraining their anger. When the time came for the beating of the drum, "boom, boom, boom," the two broke into laughter again. The guests also broke into laughter after they could no longer hold it in.

As soon as the wedding was over, the father of the groom rushed at Han Shan and Shi De in anger, as if to seize them by their throats. Han Shan and Shi De calmly smiled and explained why they were laughing. They had laughed the first time because the man's grandmother had been reincarnated as the bride and was about to become his daughter-in-law. They laughed the second time because his aunt had died and become a cow, and then died again a couple of years ago. Her leather had been used to make the drum that was used in the wedding, so they said they were laughing because the affairs of human life were so funny.

When seen by an enlightened eye, this world is a wide open field of repeated dreams and jokes. At the same time, for the ignorant, this world can be complete darkness without any sense of direction. The chain of karmic causality, however, goes forward with absolute accuracy.

Should we laugh, or should we cry?

Thirteen

At the Monastery

WHEN THE RAYS OF SPRING COME

These days, our monastery is comfortably warm, filled with the essence of spring. The bright rays of the sun are mild, and the trees and the saplings are finding new strength.

Recently, we bought five eight-year-old sweet persimmon trees and five jujube trees. As I plant the sweet persimmon trees that have come all the way from Jinyeong and the jujube trees from Daegu, my mind teems with joy. Thinking about the red persimmons and the jujubes that will be hanging between the tinted maple leaves, I am already excited. Because the sweet persimmons and the jujubes are exposed to the salty winds of the Eastern Sea, their fruit will become saltier and taste even better. Proudly standing upright among the other saplings, they have a fine look that suits the atmosphere of the monastery. I am surrendering even this beautiful scene.

When I was at Sosa, we also grew fruit trees, such as peach, plum, and pear. Fertilizing in the spring and personally pruning and covering the fruit with paper bags was such happy and meaningful work. Back then, I thought only about serving those fruits to my master. Now, as I plant the trees in my late forties, my only wish is to offer up the fruit to Buddha, who completely fills the universe. My mind is one of offering up everything to the delighted gaze of the Dharma-body Buddha, who remains full in the sky and always beams with a warm smile as I practice surrendering. It is the mind free from the discrimination of specially serving the fruits to my teacher.

At Sosa, I didn't get to plant the trees personally, for I had gone away to take care of other business, and when I returned, other practitioners had already planted them. I was disappointed. But now I harbor no such discriminating mind. I invoke a won with all my heart for whoever plants and takes care of the trees and lend my hands to him or her. People often say, "A picture of a cake." This means that only when one is actually eating cake, rather than seeing a picture of it, will one be satisfied. Even with someone else's cake, however, if you offer it up to Buddha with your mind, how delighted will he be? If you see someone else eating, how happy will you be?

Some have suggested that we plant flowers at the monastery, too. But rather than growing something that is beautiful only, a preference for trees that bear fruit may be a more spiritual practice. I would like to plant more medlar fruit trees.

Today, I tended the monastery with the young practitioners. In order to pave a new farm road behind the aromatic trees, we raised an embankment and brought in dirt to widen the road. People drove their tractors across the monastery grounds, and dogs often entered the monastery, distracting the spiritual practitioners. We planted a fence of saplings around the monastery for a boundary. We put up a fence and gates to guard the minds of spiritual seekers.

In this monastery full of pure energy, devoting my life to making Buddha happy along with young spiritual seekers, who come with selfless ideals, and receiving warm spring rays with them is indeed the truest happiness. It is said that the spiritual practitioner's chest and the green forest in the early morning give out life energy. The reason why this monastery has become more radiant and peaceful is because of Buddha's white radiance and the power of the spiritual seekers' practice. A life without greed, a life of cleansing karmic hindrances, a life of illuminating wisdom, a life of planting merit before Buddha—this is the life of pure happiness.

As we sense the vitality in the scent of the earth, we work with the intention of raising life. Then we stroll in the pine forest behind the monastery. We wake up at three in the morning, when Bodhisattva Manjushri is said to give his Dharma lecture, to read the Diamond Sutra. We live in the radiance of Buddha. This life of peace and joy can only be due to the grace of Buddha.

Soon, when April comes, the chorus of frogs in the rice paddies around the monastery will sound like the recitation of *Mireukjon Yeoraebul*. After finishing a bright and powerful practice in the evening, blissful energy arises in my lower abdomen, filling my whole body and mind with bliss. As I walk the serene monastery grounds, I feel that the Dharma-bliss of reciting *Mireukjon Yeoraebul* over and over must be the greatest happiness. Since I have been residing in this monastery for quite a while, people tell me that there seems to be a thicker fragrance around me. I surrender even this fragrance as an offering to Buddha. Whatever it is, the moment when you offer up something to Buddha is happiness.

When I was training at Sosa, I would look around as I walked out of the outer bathroom after finishing the evening practice. The warm and snug atmosphere of the valley, filled with the rays of the moon, was like that of Buddha's realm or the heaven of the immortals. I would want to savor the beauty of the harmony between the white radiance and the moonlight, but dark energy circulates after 9:00 p.m. Since it might have harmed my practice, I would close the door and hurry back to my room.

These days, the worries that I had in my twenties about not attaining enlightenment have calmed down a lot. I surrender as I calmly watch the moonlight and the bright luminescence that spreads within the reaches of the juniper trees.

THE MUD HOUSE

For some time now, practitioners at our monastery have been making a mud house. First, we dug up the mud from the mountain and mixed it with straw cut with the straw-cutter; then we compressed it in a wooden rack to make mud bricks. While they dried in the sun for about a month, we cared for them well, covering them when it rained.

We are building this mud house to use it as a drying room for *meju* (compressed blocks of bean paste that we use to make soy sauce). After we install the underfloor heating system and huge cauldrons, we'll boil the soy beans in the cauldrons using firewood, and the heat will dry the mejus. Having laid the concrete foundation, we laid about thirty centimeters of cement bricks. We are planning to build two twenty-eight-square-yard rooms. When the brick foundations have dried well, we will build up the mud bricks a couple of layers at a time.

The cement bricks that we used were also made by the practitioners two years ago. They seemed bored with nothing to do in the winter, so I ordered a brick-making machine. We built a greenhouse and made the bricks inside. At first we made some mistakes, but we made the bricks with care, all the while reciting *Mireukjon Yeoraebul*. When the two rooms started to take shape, we made girders and rafters from the acacia tree that had been cut from the mountain near our monastery, and we fastened them with wire.

In the beginning, I didn't feel very comfortable, for we had started to build the house without any previous experience. Now that the house is taking shape, I'm beginning to feel more confident. I have built two houses before, but since most of the work was done by technicians, I didn't pay much attention. I have never built a mud house before. Since most of the spiritual practitioners here had just graduated from schools or gotten out of the army when they came, they didn't know much about building houses either.

Fortunately, there was one person who had some experience. After putting him in charge of building the mud house, I told him to intensely surrender any questions he had during the early morning and evening practice times in order to receive answers about how to build the house. The one in charge gradually proceeded with the work by realizing or seeing the answers to his questions after surrendering them. His questions included the problem of laying the mud bricks, of building the underfloor heating system, of placing the girders, of pulling out the rafters, and crossing the rafters and the girders. He said that sometimes he sought expert opinions or followed common sense, but surrendering by reciting *Mireukjon Yeoraebul* had given him great wisdom. He has been studying here for about a year now. Building the house has been a good opportunity for him to plant merit, and it has also forced him to practice.

On top of the rafters and girders, we placed the wooden boards in random order. Then we mixed chopped straw, mud, and water. The practitioners mixed them by stepping on them with their bare feet. The sound of their loud recitation, while mixing up the mud, resonated throughout the monastery. Then we carried the mixture to the top of the roof. The ones who carried the mud also did not stop reciting *Mireukjon Yeoraebul*. After plastering the mud on to the wooden boards, we put the slates on top of them. It is a house made entirely of mud. A house I built in my past incarnation, by erecting a mud wall and personally cutting a tree from the mountain, must have been similar to this one.

Enlightening one's mind is like this. Whatever the task, even if you don't know how to do it or lack experience at first, if you keep learning and practicing, eventually it can be completed. Practice surrendering your deficient and incompetent states of mind. Proceed on your path by learning step by step and by practicing what you have learned. If you have no notion of not knowing, or of not being able to do something, your level of practice is probably advanced.

Lastly, we plastered the interior walls with mud, as we had done on the outside, so that there wouldn't be any wind blowing through the cracks. A fine looking house has been built, and because everyone feels good about themselves, my heart is filled with contentment.

We have started a fire in the hearth, and the floors are beginning to warm up. When we hang mejus, the mud wall will absorb all of the moisture and dry it well. I am already becoming excited, thinking that it will be a room in which to serve Buddha.

YOUNG SPIRITUAL SEEKER
AND EARLY SPRING

The first day of spring is only a few days away. The energy of the universe goes through a significant change during the change of seasons. There are two points where the biggest change of energy occurs. The first is the time when the long winter is over and spring is about to begin. The second point is when fall is about to change to winter, the time when paulownia leaves start to fall. The person whose mind is not disturbed around these points has awakened unshakable spiritual strength.

Because they live depending on the earth, a slight tremor arises in the minds of young spiritual seekers as the first day of spring approaches. It must be that the unsurrendered emotions that were buried inside throughout the winter are now sprouting to the surface, just as the orchid prepares a new bud underground, and sprouts up through the thick earth.

Since the old days, it has been said that, when spring comes, the heavy temple remains, but the light and careless monk departs. During this period, the minds of practitioners are very unstable compared to ordinary times. Their minds are full of wandering thoughts—thoughts about the world outside the monastery, thoughts about home. When that happens, usually their friends or families call or write to them. Since a novice practitioner sends out an unstable mind wave, the echo of that wave returns to give him or her a tempting answer, asking him or her to leave the monastery.

If one's mind were free of inner discriminations from the beginning, there would not be such contacts from the outside. But as a result of not being able to surrender that disturbed state of mind, a corresponding answer comes back from the people outside the monastery. If a spiritual practitioner can surrender his or her state of mind at that time, they can still free themselves from their discriminating minds. If the practitioner cannot surrender the unstable mind at that time, he or she might leave the monastery, enslaved by the unstable mind wave that he or she has created.

The mind wave that you create always returns to your heart like an echo. We cannot deny this obvious, ironclad rule. But those who strictly keep their practice times in the morning and evening, according to the precepts, do not easily become infected with spring fever. They all surrender well.

I've heard that cities are full of disturbances and accidents around the first day of spring. Automobile accidents increase in the streets, and people have more conflicts within their families or in the workplace because they cannot surrender their hatred of each other. Furthermore, since the first day of spring is before the lunar New Year's Day, the whole country is in tumult. Especially in times like these, we need people who cultivate their minds to calm their surroundings with the bright energy they generate from spiritual practice.

In the monastery, our minds are bright and clear in the morning. After three in the afternoon, people say that their minds are sad, somewhat depressed, and lonely. When a practitioner surrenders such a state of mind well at that time and goes on to do the evening practice, his or her mind will calm itself and become clearer.

We go to bed around 9:30 in the evening and wake up to begin our spiritual practice at 2:40 in the morning, when the radiant energy is brewing in the universe. Therefore, we are surrounded by the life energy, and in that refreshing energy, our karmic hindrances melt away as they arise.

While working during the day, whenever aversion to work or fatigue arises, we surrender such feelings at that very moment. Looking into our minds all day long and surrendering the arising thoughts and emotions, there isn't a moment when reciting *Mireukjon Yeoraebul* stops. Here and there, all over the monastery, you can hear them reciting *Mireukjon Yeoraebul*. Perhaps they have forgotten the fact that they are sitting on a toilet, but I sometimes hear people reciting Buddha's name in the bathrooms!

To completely solve the problem of repeated birth and death, these practitioners have been preparing a good environment in which to pursue the spiritual practice. Cultivating one's mind is indeed an important task. However, since there is no medicine that can cure one's innate nature, it is a difficult task indeed to change one's habitual mind.

When hidden karmic hindrances from many former lifetimes arise, some practitioners surrender continually for three hours in the *jang-gwe* position, in addition to our normal practice hours. To surrender the attachment that has risen in their minds, some people even sacrifice their sleep. Though I am sympathetic, their efforts to solve their problems by surrendering them one by one seem fierce.

Why have they, in their youth, rejected all other easy and comfortable ways to follow this path? Why are they working in the rough fields, exposed to cold winds, with no experience of farming? Why are they working in the mill, planting merit and living frugal lives? Their efforts to become enlightened, while forsaking money, fame, and pleasure, might not make sense to ordinary people. I suppose it is because they are the reincarnations of spiritual practitioners who have been cultivating the path for many incarnations.

Some twenty years ago, when I was practicing at Sosa, I often cut wood for fuel on the mountain in the winter by myself. In the desolate hills where all the leaves had fallen, cold gusts of wind would blow. The tips of my hands and feet would freeze, and become numb. On the days when even the sky was grimacing, it was especially scary, and I would recite *Mireukjon Yeoraebul* to overcome my fear until my vocal cords were about to burst.

While going through pain and inner discord, there were many days when I was sick of life at Sosa. When the pain was unbearable, I practiced surrendering and told myself that I hadn't been born in this life [trying to convince myself that it was not real]. Still, I spent my seven and a half years at Sosa worrying about not becoming enlightened in this life. To purify the attachment to one's body is painful. Why must we cultivate our minds through such hardships? I suppose it is the dilemma of everyone who tries to become enlightened.

As Master Baek said, the former Indian prime minister, Jawaharlal Nehru, is a being that appears only once every five hundred years in this world, Gandhi is one who appears only once every thousand years, and Shakyamuni Buddha is one who appears only once every three thousand years. In order to become like Nehru, like Ghandi, and like Shakyamuni Buddha, even today, in this monastery, there are young spiritual seekers planting merit and illuminating their wisdom. Won't the future of the realm of sentient beings become brighter because of such people? It isn't coincidental that some people witness the radiance of Buddha in these young seekers, who reverently serve Buddha while forsaking the conveniences of modern civilization.

To solve the problem of eternal birth and death and to spread brightness to many people by serving Buddha, we should gradually cultivate our minds. Outside my room, where I am writing this book, many voices making offerings to Buddha are spreading high and wide into the rays of the afternoon sun.

F o u r t e e n

Path of the Bodhisattva

This chapter contains Dharma lectures intended to help
the practitioners practice the Bodhisattva Mind, Bodhisattva Act,
and Bodhisattva Path, together with specific examples of
how these practices were carried out in daily life.

MAY YOU PLANT GREAT MERIT IN THE NEW YEAR

In Korea, as the New Year approaches, people exchange seasonal greetings by saying "May you receive good fortune in the New Year." We cannot receive good fortune, however, if we have not planted merit, nor can we gain wisdom if we have not cultivated the mind. The common greeting to "receive good fortune" is simply empty words.

In the case of a person who does not practice charity or has not planted merit, or who disregards, despises, and speaks badly of others, and lives a corrupt and immoral life, it is meaningless to say "May you receive good fortune." We should rather say "May you plant great merit in the New Year," if our words are to be meaningful.

Wisdom arises by cultivating the mind, and good fortune accumulates by planting merit.

KIND INTENTIONS WILL RETURN TO YOU

In Korea, there is a saying, "One kind word returns another." (*lit.* "When kind words go, kind words come.") More important than words, however, is the intention behind the words. The mind must be well-intentioned in order for the "mind" that comes back to be well-intentioned as well.

When I see someone as my Buddha and treat him or her with respect, because my mind toward the person is respectful, the other person will give back a respectful mind, according to the wave that my own mind has sent out. When I regard someone with hatred, as my hateful mind's waves ripple outwards, the other person's own hatred will echo back to me with a higher degree of intensity. The mind that others practice towards me is a response to the one I send out to them.

We might practice the mindset of seeing others as Buddha as a means of changing the way we view other people. However, the purpose is also to practice reverence in our own mind. When we practice a reverent and respectful mind by seeing others as Buddha, it enriches and cultivates our mind like watering a field. The mindset of those who cultivate the mind is one of constant reverence.

THE ROOT OF SUFFERING

Although they do not say it out loud, people often harbor expectations of others. The husband has unspoken expectations of his wife, and the wife has unspoken expectations of her husband. Children expect to receive things from their parents, just as the parents expect to receive things from their children. Whenever expectations are unfulfilled, people grow angry inside and the relationship sours.

When you have many expectations of those around you, the world becomes a bitter and frustrating place. The mind that wants something from others is at the root of suffering.

We must surrender constantly in order to be freed from this mind. When the mind that wants something arises, reawaken the thought "I should not generate the mind of want," and cleanse the mind to its very roots by reading the Diamond Sutra and reciting *Mireukjon Yeoraebul* to that mind. When you are not burdened by expectations, you will be confident and happy, and your mind will be cheerful.

By surrendering the expecting and needy mind, devote yourself to your tasks instead of leaning on others. If you put your whole mind and effort into the task at hand, you will be able to accomplish your goal. How pleasant it is to be able to achieve one's tasks without relying on others!

The craving, needy mind is the root of all suffering. Therefore, we should cleanse our minds of want and expectation to become liberated from them altogether, and instead practice the healthy mind of helping and giving to others.

THE DHARMA LECTURE OF THE POINTING FINGER

We often point our fingers at others when we find fault with them. However, if we look we will see that although the index finger is pointing at the other person, the middle finger, fourth finger, and little finger are pointing back at us. When we catch ourselves finding fault with someone, we should repent and correct three of our own faults.

You cannot cultivate another person's mind. Instead of criticizing and trying to teach others, you must look at yourself, repent and cultivate your own mind. This is the Dharma lecture of the pointing finger.

MY FAULT

The three poisons of the mind are greed, anger, and arrogance. These poisons cause people to hurt and harm others. However, because they do not see the poison in their own minds, people complain that they are upset because of the poison in other people's minds. Those who blame themselves, rather than others, are advanced in their spiritual practice.

You should be wary of such thoughts as "Because of this person" or "Because of someone else" and promptly surrender them. You can only practice humility when you realize that everything is your fault and a result of the causes you have planted. Those who find the causes of their misfortunes in themselves will succeed and progress in their study. Those who blame and resent others wander far from the path of spiritual practice.

Even if someone criticizes us, if we think to ourselves, "He must be doing this because my karmic hindrances are deep, and because the karmic hindrances in my mind are sending out negative energy," the problem is no longer with the other person. Quarrels occur and conflicts arise because the energy of our karmic hindrances is transmitted from our mind. They occur because we stubbornly refuse to yield to others, having nurtured our ego for so long without being able to cleanse it. Ultimately, all causes lie within us.

A BOULDER

Whether it rains or snows, whether it is praised or blamed, a boulder remains silent and motionless. If the boulder were to lose patience, or clash and fight with other rocks, it would break into fragments and become pebbles. Its value and strength would disappear.

A rock is precious because it stays calm and silent. Whatever words of compliment or criticism it hears, it does not waver.

The silence of a rock, its faithfulness and constancy, is something a practitioner should emulate both in attitude and mind.

PRACTICING THE BRIGHT MIND

Buddha said that there is an eternal treasure in our body called the "mind." Depending on how it is used, this precious treasure of the mind will bring happiness or misfortune. We should therefore surrender the negative minds we have practiced for many lifetimes, and try to practice positive minds every day, even if it feels empty or forced. This way, our lives can take a positive turn.

The mind that reveres Lord Buddha, the mind that lowers itself and thinks highly of others, the mind that gives generously and puts others first—this positive mind wave comes back to you like an echo. This echo, a result of the bright, wholesome mind, is merit and good fortune. The negative mind wave that returns to you after practicing dark minds is disaster and misfortune.

A single mind determines not only the life of one person, but also the future of the family he or she lives with, and the future of the nation where such people live together.

If the mentality of a nation is that of respecting the rule of law and living with honesty, humility, and thrift, this will form the basis of a greater merit, and the nation's fortunes will improve. If the mentality of people is that of disregarding the law, living with dishonesty and arrogance, extravagance and waste, then that nation's fortunes will decline. The minds of a nation's people converge to determine its fate.

When the mind changes, the fate of an individual, the future of a family, and the destiny of a nation all change. The mind is the center of all.

REALIZATION AND PRACTICE

Farmers cultivate pear trees to harvest their fruits, not to admire their blossoms. It is the same for those who cultivate the mind. The moment you realize "This is how I should live," "This is how I should cultivate the mind," you must put it into practice from that moment onwards.

Those who study well and who have deep good-roots attain realizations by themselves, but such cases are rare. For most people, moments of realization come through listening to Dharma lectures. Whether you have realized something by yourself or through a Dharma lecture, the moment you realize it, you must put it into practice straightaway. Simply realizing something and not practicing it is like admiring the blossom without picking the fruit.

Without practice, the realizations that one has are no more than a useless theory, and they will never become part of us. Only those who put their realizations into practice can harvest the fruits of their study.

AFTER DEATH THAT IS NOT FAR AWAY, WHAT BODY WILL I RECEIVE?

Venerable Ananda was one of the ten great disciples of the Buddha. One day, as he sat meditating quietly, a mosquito landed on his cheek. He tried to wave it away, and killed it by mistake.

Venerable Ananda placed the dead mosquito on his palm, and prayed for it to be reborn in the Pure Land. As he prayed, he looked into its past lives. Two lives ago, the mosquito had been a mighty general in India, with power and influence that stretched across the land. He was oppressive to the weak, however, and weak before the strong. In particular, he was known for his excessive flattery of the king. As a result, in his next incarnation, he had to live as a prostitute, and in the life after that, he became a mosquito and fed off the blood of others.

When a powerful general, who ruled over the vast lands of India, could become a mosquito in his next life, how can anyone be confident of receiving a human body in his or her next life? A life spent in quest of the Five Pleasures, a life devoted solely to the pursuit of wealth, sexual desire, fame, delicious food and sleep—what body is in store for such a person in the future? Therefore, we should offer up our inner discriminations to the bright radiance of Buddha, and accumulate virtue and charitable deeds. How could this not be urgent?

THE WEIGHING SCALES OF OUR CONSCIENCE

One's future is determined by the good and bad deeds one carries out in one's lifetime. Those who perform many good deeds and who have planted virtue will receive a bright future, while those who have committed many sins will have a dark fate.

In the past, when there were no other opportunities for good deeds, enlightened masters would plant merit by cutting grass and feeding their neighbors' cattle. If they saw ivy climbing a tree, they cut it down to save the tree and plant merit. They went to help orphaned children, and carried luggage for the elderly. Enlightened masters always try to do several good deeds like this every day.

We too must live our lives so that the scales of our conscience are balanced in favor of good deeds and not bad ones. If you hurt another person's feelings with your words, tell a lie or do something wrong, then before the end of the day, you should make sure that your good deeds outnumber the bad ones by picking up litter in the park, taking meals to orphaned children, cleaning the communal areas of your apartment and so on.

CLEANING THE MONASTERY

Since they have been washing dishes, wiping floors and cleaning their homes for many years, many bosallims feel it is tedious to do the same tasks at the monastery as well. Cleaning the house and cleaning the monastery are different, however. The house is a place of rest for your body while the monastery is a place of rest for your mind, where you enshrine Buddha and cultivate the mind, a place where you remove the mind's impurities. Virtue is planted when you clean and look after such a precious place with devotion and care.

MODESTY IS THE GREATEST VIRTUE

People who lower themselves, reflect on their own faults, and practice the mind of learning from others are rare indeed. Of the seven billion human beings in the world, most people either praise themselves or criticize others whenever they open their mouths. Although this happens because they are full of arrogance, people are often unaware how much arrogance exists in their minds, because they are lacking in wisdom.

Practice thinking "I am the lowest person in the world" ten thousand times a day. Through the practice of lowering yourself, you will be awakened to your boastful and deluded state of mind. As such notions are cleansed, we come to realize that there is nothing great about us after all. The more we practice the mind of lowering ourselves, the more we see—both close up and from afar—the aspects of ourselves that are flawed. Because we are persistent in seeing that flawed self, we will lower ourselves even more. In the end, we will awaken from the mindset that is blinded by arrogance and be freed from it. Then, we will commit fewer sins, and have the mindset of learning from others and seeking their advice.

There is nothing more precious than humility. A humble mind fills its surroundings with warmth. How fragrant is the gentle and unassuming smile, how noble and worthy is the countenance and footstep of a humble individual. If you keep lowering yourself, a warm energy will spread to your surroundings, and good things will befall you.

THE PRACTICE OF LOWERING ONESELF

If I think highly of myself, my life will be difficult. When I meet someone, I feel that I should be treated well and be complimented, and I must somehow show off the little that I have. The medicine that cures the disease of ignorance and the delusion that "I am great," is the practice of thinking "I am a lowly person." Members of the Diamond Sutra Recitation Group take this medicine a thousand or ten thousand times a day, keeping a tally of how many times they practice this mind by holding and pressing a counter in their hand.

When you lower yourself, your ego calms. You realize your faults and shortcomings. People who do not surrender their delusion of self-importance go through life insisting, "Listen to me. Do as I say. Be like me." Because of their arrogance, they do not see the precious qualities in others, but only their faults. Moreover, by judging and criticizing others with their mind, they commit *sim-eop* (mental sins). Without being aware of it, they commit these sins hundreds of times a day.

Once again, the way to avoid committing sim-eop is to practice thinking "I am a lowly person." If we cultivate our mind in this way, we can at least find out who we really are. If I truly am a lowly being, how could I criticize anyone? Whom can I teach and whom can I judge?

There is nothing as difficult as lowering yourself. This is because, for countless lives, we have practiced raising ourselves until it has become like a chronic disease. As we look down on others, others also look down on us, even though no one knows it.

This is the trap of ignorance. We must first realize this: if we were really as great as we think, people from our country and other countries would visit us to pay their respects. If this is not the case, we must realize that the notions we hold about ourselves are incorrect. At this very moment, your family, friends and work colleagues probably think that you are worth less than they are.

Lowering yourself is the key and the foundation of our study. If we do not lower ourselves, we are separated from the world of wisdom, and traveling in the opposite direction of enlightenment. As Master Wonhyo said, you prepare a meal by cooking rice, but someone who tries to cultivate the mind without lowering himself is like a person trying to prepare a meal with sand. However hard you try, one cannot prepare a meal of rice with sand. Only when you lower yourself and generate the mindset of learning from others can wisdom arise.

ASK THE EXPERTS

Wise people never make important decisions by themselves, but first seek the advice of an expert. The best way of approaching a task is by seeking advice from the most knowledgeable person in the field. Many people, however, do not seek the advice of others. Because of delusions about their own ability and importance, they feel too ashamed to ask. Making a decision by oneself on the spur of the moment—divorced from knowledge, experience and wisdom—could easily open the door to error and failure.

Since you are faced with many decisions in life—starting a business, finding a spouse or providing a good education for your children—consult a specialist in that field first. It is even better if you consult three experts and not just one person. Once you have listened to their advice, do not simply follow it to the letter, but pray for at least twenty-one days on the issue. If you then make a careful decision, you will suffer less from trial and error, and the likelihood of failure will be lessened.

Whether in spiritual practice, business, or education, you will succeed when you lower yourself and then do your best.

THE FRAGRANCE OF VIRTUE

> The fragrance of rosebay or sandalwood does not
> spread against the wind,
> But the fragrance of virtue spreads on every side,
> regardless of the wind.
>
> Dhammapada Sutra

The scent of a flower spreads only in the direction of the wind, as it is a physical phenomenon. But the spiritual scent and fragrance of virtue accumulated in the mind spreads in all directions.

In Korean, someone who has accumulated great merit is called a "full" person, while someone who has accumulated virtue is a "fulfilled" person, and one with wisdom is a "fair" person. You plant merit by helping and giving to others, and wisdom develops by being humble, lowering yourself, and having the mindset of learning from others.

To accumulate virtue, you must be able to hold your tongue. Virtue will not grow when you find faults in others and argue over the right or wrong of their situation. Virtue will blossom when you practice the mindset of covering up the faults of others as if they were your own, and uncovering your own faults as if they were the faults of others. Virtue also grows in the mind that puts others before oneself and tries to understand them.

SCHOLAR KIM JIP

Kim Jip was a prominent Neo-Confucian scholar under King Hyojong of Joseon, and unequaled in his understanding of Confucian rites and etiquette. He was a student of Master Yulgok. Master Yulgok had a close friend whose daughter was mentally retarded. One day, the friend visited the Master and pleaded with him in earnest.

"Only a man of great virtue or enlightened wisdom could accept my daughter as his wife. No ordinary person could do it. If you know of anyone suitable among your students, please introduce him to me."

A few days later, Master Yulgok gathered his students together and announced, "I will serve lunch for you tomorrow, so do not bring food with you."

The students were excited, believing that their teacher was going to treat them to a banquet. But when they sat down for lunch the next day, plain dishes of boiled barley and bitter lettuce soup were set before them. Since most of the students came from wealthy families, this sort of food was unfamiliar to them. So no one ate except Kim Jip, who alone finished all his food.

"Doesn't it taste bitter?"

"It is bitter, but it is food given by my teacher. Therefore I must eat it all."

Greatly esteeming his student, Master Yulgok told him to marry the daughter of his friend.

Some years later, an ancestral rite was being held at Kim Jip's household. Suddenly, his wife tugged at his sleeve and asked him to take a dried date from the altar and give it to her. Hastily, Kim Jip gave the date to his wife.

In those days, ancestral rites were solemn religious ceremonies. Those taking part had to bathe to purify the body beforehand, and the proceedings were held in reverent silence. This incident happened as the altar was being prepared. Seeing this, the senior members of the family scolded him.

"You are a scholar held in the highest regard by all of our country's learned men, and yet you break with custom, giving your wife food intended for your ancestors even before the ceremony has begun!"

Kim Jip replied. "How could I be unaware of this? The ceremony is an occasion for us to honor and attend upon our ancestors. If the family offers up the ceremony in peace and harmony together, I believe that our ancestors will be pleased. But if my wife is angry or sheds tears because of one dried date, would our ancestors not be displeased, visiting us after a long period of absence? This is why I quickly gave her the fruit. The situation arose because I am lacking in virtue. Please forgive my faults."

Hearing his words, the senior members of the family greatly admired him.

Kim Jip was a renowned scholar who achieved success through his mastery of the Confucian rites and customs. His success was thanks to his cultivation of the mind. Because of his lacking wife, he developed patience and became capable of suffering and endurance, with a mindset of lowering himself ceaselessly. He also received an unrelenting spiritual training through his academic studies. His wife would have been unable to educate the children, or handle the housekeeping or cooking.

However, by enduring the sufferings of a difficult life, Kim Jip found success.

A SPIRITUAL LEGACY FOR FUTURE GENERATIONS

In the mid-Joseon dynasty, there lived a man called Kim Chang-saeng. As he was preparing cuts of pork for an ancestral ceremony one day, he left the kitchen for a few moments. His dog ate some of the pork, then let out a loud bark and died shortly afterwards. It was clear that the pork had spoiled. When he saw this, Chang-saeng sent a man to the butcher's shop to buy all of the meat in stock, and had it buried at a place far away from the village.

An ordinary person would probably have asked the butcher for compensation for the death of his dog. As a member of the aristocracy, Chang-saeng could have had the lowly man arrested and beaten as a punishment. Instead, he purchased everything at the butcher's shop with his own money and buried it to ensure that no one else would buy the stale meat. He thereby protected not only the health and lives of the villagers, but also the butcher himself. Through the merit of his generosity, his household and family won great respect throughout the nation, and subsequently produced many distinguished individuals.

Sang Yeong-bu, a wealthy man from the Imcheon region, practiced virtue in his daily life and gained universal esteem by lending money to those who needed it urgently. On New Year's Eve, he took out all the papers from his safe relating to loans and sureties, and made a bonfire of them in his back garden. Seeing the smoke rise to the sky gave him an incomparable joy. People across the country said that his descendants would benefit from his virtuous deeds, and he later had a grandson called Sang Jin, a famous prime minister who served under King Myeongjong.

In the Hahwe village of Andong, there is a beautiful ancestral estate called Bukchon-daek. Built in the traditional way upon one-point-four acres of land and containing seventy-two rooms, its owners enjoyed great wealth and honor in the Yeongnam region for seven generations and over two hundred years. The person who built this house was Ryu Do-seong, who served as the governor of Gyeongsang Province and was the tenth lineal descendant of Ryu Seong-ryong, another distinguished prime minister of Joseon.

Late one evening, a ferry carrying many people back to the Hahwe village was overturned. The party had crossed the river earlier in the day to give their condolences at a mourning house, and the boat capsized owing to a sudden rise in the water level.

As street lamps or flashlights did not exist in those days, they were surrounded by darkness on every side. Caught in the middle of the river, the survivors paddled desperately and shouted for help, but there was no boat in sight that could come to their rescue. However, there happened to be by the riverside some piles of well-seasoned diamond pine. Ryu Do-seong had been drying the rare and expensive timber for three years in order to build his villa.

Seeing the commotion, he threw some of the logs into the water to be used as lifeboats, and set the rest on fire to provide a light to see by. In doing so he saved many lives. Afterwards, he managed with difficulty to obtain more of the rare diamond pine logs, and once again dried them for three years. These were the timbers used to build what later became the beautiful villa of Bukchon-daek.

Prominent families in Korea shared their wealth with the poor, lived in humility, and practiced charity in secret. Because their descendents have inherited such precious, benevolent traditions of life and, because of the power of their ancestors' merit, their families continue to be prominent and prosperous today. As we live our lives today, should we not also leave behind such spiritual legacies for our children and the youth of tomorrow?

EGO

When people look at family photographs, whose face do they look at first? It is said that everyone looks at their own faces first. Even if the picture contains a spouse one is devoted to, or children one loves, the way of the human mind is to be interested in oneself first, and one's spouse or children second.

What does this mean? It implies that what matters most to us is ourselves, whereas our children, husband and wife are of secondary importance. We say that we work for the family and look after the house, but what comes first and matters to us more than husband, wife, children, or relatives is ourselves. Having lived for ourselves for countless eons, it is perhaps only natural that our minds should work this way.

However, most people are unaware of the true nature of the ego inside us—how deep-rooted and fundamental it is to our being, how it affects us, and how selfish it is in living for itself only. Parents invariably say that they live for their children but, in many cases, they are in fact seeking to satisfy themselves through their children. Although they say that it is for their children, ultimately they are living for themselves.

Only by cleansing the ego that is bound by the notion of "I" can one truly live for others, and truly love oneself. Through the practice of lowering oneself and not imposing oneself on others, and the practice of living for Buddha—the ego melts away.

Lower yourself. Practice reverence towards Buddha. Practice the teachings of Buddha. This practice must become part of your daily life, and part of your character. Just as the great pear tree bears much delicious fruit, you must persevere in the journey of your eternal soul's enlightenment, until it bears a fruitful outcome.

THE MINDSET OF PRACTICE

A spiritual practitioner must follow the monastic rules and live a pure life. While following the rules with dedication is commendable, if the basis is not to serve Buddha, then it is no more than restricting oneself with precepts. What drives our spiritual practice forward is reverence towards Buddha and the mindset of serving Buddha. If the mindset of your practice is "I will become enlightened," "I will follow the rules," "I will plant merit," and not serving Buddha, then you will run into difficulty.

People are often concerned with who is following the rules, who can maintain the lotus position longest without lying down, who has recited for the longest amount of time, and so on. The greatest issue is whether the mind has reverence for Buddha, but unfortunately this is often forgotten.

Since Buddha is not visible to the eyes, the initial method of practice is to think of our teacher or the people we respect as Buddhas. After practicing like this, we might then try the method of directing our mind to the Dharmakaya Buddha. We could also believe and practice the mindset that everyone we meet is an incarnation of Shakyamuni Buddha who has come to this world to help us with our practice.

We have to practice reverence towards Buddha in order for our karmic hindrances to melt away. When karmic hindrances are eradicated, our basic consciousness becomes clear of obstacles, and as the consciousness clears, the wisdom-eye will open. Because the karmic hindrances and karmic ties that we have accumulated over eons will not melt away unless reverence arises within us, we practice seeing others as Buddha. Unless the karmic hindrances and karmic ties are removed, our spiritual practice is merely superficial.

However little you sleep, however long you fast, however many hours you recite in the lotus position without lying down, it is all for nothing if there is no Buddha in your mind. Even if we were to eat frugally and refrain from lying down for tens of years, without reverence to Buddha we are living an austere life and nothing more. While ascetic practices like this might make the body feel lighter and clear the mind, they will not lead us to true virtue and will not eradicate our karmic hindrances. It is only through practicing reverence to Buddha that our karmic hindrances and deeply-ingrained habits will melt away and our mind will become enlightened.

Before your life's purpose, and after your life's purpose, Buddha must be present always.

PEOPLE WHO TRULY LOVE THEMSELVES

Although everyone lives for himself or herself and for his or her own gain, people who love themselves are rare in this world. What does this mean?

People who live for themselves love their bodily attachments and the Five Desires (wealth, lust, fame, delicious food and sleep) and nothing more. Although it will soon decay, people are constantly running errands for their physical bodies.

People who truly love themselves are those who have regard for their pure soul, their bright mind, and their true nature, which is as clear as crystal. Without being able to love the mind and soul, many live in the mistaken belief that loving and nurturing their bodies alone is the way to lead a good life. This is the reality for many people. If your love for the body and the Five Desires is strong, you will not be able to love those around you.

It is the people who surrender the ego and bodily attachments, and the people who love their soul and mind, who truly love themselves. Only those who truly love themselves are able to love their family, neighbors, and their country. To love one's country means to love its land and the many people who live on it, as well as its history and the cultural legacies of the ancestors.

Although there are many people in this country, there are very few who truly love and are concerned for their nation. "I must do well," "I must get more," "I must succeed"—those who live solely for their own benefit and greed are not capable of loving their country.

RETRIBUTIVE KARMIC TIES

Some years ago, there was a woman who was mistreated by her husband from the first night of their marriage. Such was the extent of her hardship that when she carefully made new clothes for him to wear, he would scowl and hurl them into a bucket of dirty water. When she prepared meals for him, he would complain "What food do you call this?" and kick away the table. Needless to say, he was also unfaithful to her in marriage. She told me that her whole life had been this way.

There is an old Confucian teaching that a wife should not desert her household, and remain there even in death as a spirit. However, the real reason she did not leave, although she did not know it, was because of a single mind which endured the karmic retribution and said—"He treats me harshly now, but he will bury me in a warm place when I am gone…"

The karmic tie of the couple is said to have been as follows. In a past life, the wife was a stepmother, and the husband was her stepson. On an icy day in winter, when they were alone together, the stepmother stripped the eight-year-old son bare, hit him with a sharp, thorny rod and drove him out of the house. The beaten and banished son of her past life was now her husband in this life, and because of his resentment towards her, which had grown immeasurably greater during his past life, he mistreated her from the very first night of their marriage. Between spouses, siblings, parents, and children, there are cases in which the invisible ropes of karmic retribution tie people together just like this.

Take care of your mind, words, and actions by being prudent

and sincere, so as not to incur the resentment of others. As you are receiving the karmic retribution for which you have planted the causes, if you read the Diamond Sutra, surrender and truly repent, then it is possible to be freed from the effects a little sooner. Many times I have heard women say, "My husband used to treat me so badly when we were younger, and now that he is old and weak, even his complaining has become less frequent." Because the karmic debt has been paid off, the relationship has naturally become peaceful.

The scriptures provide the following analogy to describe how difficult it is to receive a human body. Imagine a wooden board with a hole in it, drifting on the vast expanse of the sea. In the water there lives a turtle that comes to the surface every hundred years. The likelihood of receiving a human body, the scriptures explain, is the same as the likelihood of the turtle's head rising through the hole in the wooden board, on the exact occasion that it comes to the surface every century.

Being born as a human being is an extremely rare occurrence. When we receive a body, it is usually an animal's body, and sometimes we receive the same animal body for several consecutive lives. It might be the body of a viper or a serpent that we are repeatedly born into. Very occasionally, we might be born as a human being, but even then we exhibit the same tendencies and habits that we practiced as animals in the past. Rather than being formed in childhood, often our personality and behavior are based on what we have carried over from our past lives.

Watch how a sparrow constantly moves its eyes, fearful of being attacked by a larger animal. A cow, on the other hand, is never hurried and always naïve. The wily serpent might alter its course or turn back when it meets a stronger adversary, but a viper charges forward without any hesitation. Rabbits and deer are always anxious and afraid. Even when we are born as human beings, we continue to exhibit the distinctive traits that we have practiced while living as animals for countless lifetimes.

To change our narrow, weak character into a bright and

wholesome one; to finally change our ignorant way of living as we please to one of living by the teachings of Buddha, we need determination and courage. If we fail to change and solve these problems now, we will go back to living with the same faults and karmic hindrances in countless future lives, and commit the same sins, plant the same negative karma and suffer the same misfortunes as before. Some call the traits that they have been conditioned to after countless lives of practice ideologies, philosophies, and perspectives on life—but this is a foolishness that must be awakened from.

Becoming like the Buddha and following the example of his positive, healthy mind is the goal of spiritual practice and the purpose of our study. We must change our mentality to that of the Buddha. Buddha would never have said or done anything sinful, nor would he have used his mind to sin. Never committing sins, he would have lowered himself and lived in humility. He would have cared for others and comforted the weak. This was the Buddha's path, guiding many to enlightenment through the practice of cultivating the mind.

Revere Buddha and do not sin. Live honestly, lower yourself and learn from others, comforting the needy with your warmth and sharing your love with the world. This is the way to lead a blessed life.

SPOTTED SLEEPER FISH

In the upper parts of the Han River flowing through Seoul, there lives a freshwater fish called the Spotted Sleeper.

The current is strong in the center of the river and weak at the sides. After selecting a spot which it can defend against predators, the sleeper lays its eggs between the rocks by the river bank. Once the female sleeper has laid its many eggs on the rocks, they are fertilized by the male sleeper. It takes twenty days for the eggs to hatch and for the fish to develop fins. Three female sleepers lay about five thousand eggs in a single place, and these eggs require a very large amount of oxygen to survive.

The duty of the male sleeper is to protect the eggs from predators, while supplying oxygen to the eggs by moving its fins in a fan-like motion to increase the flow of oxygenated water. Without eating for twenty days and never once pausing for rest, the adult sleeper moves its fins day and night. Meanwhile the eggs hatch, and once their fins have developed, the young depart in search of food.

Once the final egg has hatched and the newborn fish have all left the area, the malnourished male sleeper sinks among the rocks and dies of exhaustion. Sacrificing everything it has for the birth and the nourishment of its young, it is the ultimate example of fatherly love.

If the sleeper wanted to preserve its life, it would be unable to accomplish its task. Seeing the protection of its five thousand young as its sole duty and destiny, it dies on the spot when its task is over. It ends its life in accordance with the laws of nature.

EMPTYING IS THE PRACTICE

"There should be few words in the mouth, few matters in the mind, and little food inside the stomach". These are the words of an enlightened master related in *The Tale of a Mind at Ease*.

As the scriptures explain, the mouth is "the gate of misfortune," and it is easy to commit *Gu-eop* (sins committed with the mouth) by talking a lot. Harsh words may strike at someone's heart like a dagger and incur their deep resentment, and one misspoken word can undo a whole virtuous deed. A spiritual practitioner should talk less and carefully watch his or her inner world for the things that need to be cleansed from the mind.

To have few matters in the mind means to calm the mind by surrendering our thoughts and ponderings, rather than brood on discriminative thoughts at length. It means to live according to our mind and spirit, rather than according to our thoughts and ponderings. If you think too much, it will lead to malice, and malice always leads to misfortune. Do not lose yourself in thoughts or ruminations, and do not be ruled by them. Instead, surrender them to empty your mind. This practice is called the cultivation of the mind.

You only need a little food inside the stomach for your body and mind to be light and healthy. Even though it feeds on wholesome grains, a hen's feathers are drab and dark because it fills its stomach full. A crane may feed on worms and insects, but its feathers are white and clean because it keeps its stomach half-full. Over-nutrition is a danger to one's health, and gives rise to lust. Spiritual seekers should therefore keep their mind and body pure and healthy by moderating their intake of food.

Cultivating the mind means constantly emptying it—clearing from our mind the three poisons of greed, anger, and arrogance through the practice of giving, reciting *Mireukjon Yeoraebul*, and lowering ourselves. Instead of rising above others, triumphing over others, and seeking more than others, respect them, consider their needs, and yield to them. Empty and lower yourself in this way—for such is the cultivation of the mind.

THE DIFFERENCE BETWEEN
A BODHISATTVA AND A SENTIENT BEING

What is the difference between a bodhisattva and a sentient being?

Sentient beings fear the result, and bodhisattvas fear the cause. Oblivious to the fact that their actions are sinful, ignorant sentient beings commit sins recklessly and without fear. It is only when they receive retribution for their sins that they experience fear and pain. The wise bodhisattva is aware of how terrible the retribution for sins can be, and both fears and guards against the causes of sin.

Sentient beings have cunning, but bodhisattvas have wisdom. For their gain and bodily comfort, sentient beings use their wits and guile. Concerned for the safety and health of others, bodhisattvas use their wisdom to help and benefit many, while sacrificing and forgoing those benefits themselves.

Those who live for themselves by cunning plant the karma of new sins every day, while those who help many with their wisdom plant virtue. Instead of a wily pursuit of personal gain, living for the benefit of many by practicing Bodhisattva Acts with the Bodhisattva Mind is the path to eternal enlightenment.

HOUSEKEEPING OF THE MIND

1. Cover up the faults of others as if they were your own, and look for faults in yourself as if they were faults in others.

2. When you see a fault in someone else, realize that it is your own fault you are seeing.

3. Practice the mind of seeing others as Buddha.

4. Practice the positive mind of saying "yes" to whatever anyone says.

5. Practice the mind of giving to everyone you meet.

6. Practice the mind of offering up your arising minds to Buddha by reciting *Mireukjon Yeoraebul*.

Let's practice the thought, "I am the lowest person in the world." When we look into our mind, there is little desire to learn from others, but much desire to teach others. This is because we are lacking in modesty and humility. If we think highly of ourselves, we tell others "Be like me," "Listen to me," "Do as I say."

As we live, let us consider the position of others and be understanding, and help those in need. Let us refrain from telling lies, and live a pure, honest life. Let us not put our interests above those of our family members, and let others have what is good before we do. We must practice good deeds every day, so that the scale of conscience is balanced in favor of our good deeds and not bad ones.

* The above is what Master Kim reads out and asks the congregation to practice at every Dharma meeting.

F i f t e e n

To Practitioners

This chapter contains words of advice given by Master Kim to
his students while checking the progress of their study.

LOOK BACK ON YOURSELF

In the *Caigentan* (lit. *Vegetable Roots Discourse*), it says "For those who look back on themselves, everything that happens to them becomes like medicine or acupuncture. For those who blame others, every thought is like a spear or a sword."

When you clash with others in your life, you should examine yourself. Consider that you may have gone too far, or made a mistake. You need to acknowledge and correct your faults and limitations while yielding to others by being sensitive to their circumstances.

If you always push as hard as you can, because of the mind-wave you give out, others will push back as hard as they can. Because you push, they push back, and because you push with arrogance, you clash with others and conflict arises. The problem will disappear if you look carefully at your own actions, lower yourself, and act considerately towards others. This is how you live in harmony with those around you, and how you grow mature and develop wisdom.

DO NOT BECOME INDEBTED

Only a handful of spiritual organizations in the world are economically self-sufficient, and this (the Diamond Sutra Recitation Group) is one of them. Because you earn your own living by farming and making traditional foods—meju, sesame oil, perilla oil, soy bean paste, chili pepper paste, and fermented soy bean—you need not depend on, or worry about, donations from lay followers. How lucky are you to be living a life of planting merit instead. In every incarnation that I devoted myself to spiritual practice, I lived my life without being indebted.

Once, an enlightened master received four packs of cold medicine, and wanting to repay that debt, he looked for the person whenever he recalled it. He searched for twenty years, but to the master's deepest regret, the person could not be found, having perhaps gone abroad. If you are indebted, or owe someone something, then you must give back as much as you have received.

THE HONESTY OF A PRACTITIONER

People who cultivate the mind must be sure that their inside and outside are the same, their start and end are the same, and that they live honestly. When you revere the Heavens, revere Buddha, serve and devote yourself to the monastery, your ego and karmic hindrances melt away. If you are self-centered, you only commit sins.

The Diamond Sutra says, "A spiritual seeker who has truly mastered the state of no-ego, according to the Tathagata, is a true bodhisattva."

A spiritual seeker who has mastered the Dharma of "no I"— someone who reveres the Heavens and serves Buddha instead of looking to further *my* study, plant *my* merit or grow *my* Dharma-power is, as the Tathagata explained, a true bodhisattva. Practicing this teaching is the honest and truthful mindset of a practitioner.

By putting yourself lower than lay followers and fellow practitioners, by giving beneficial things to others and accepting unpleasant things for yourself, by never forgoing reverence to the Heavens or Buddha and maintaining this mindset under all life's conditions, only then will the mind be cleansed and you will practice the teaching that states "a spiritual seeker who has truly mastered the state of no-ego, according to the Tathagata, is a true bodhisattva." Otherwise your study is no more than a charade.

Always speak well of others, and even if they are bad, do not speak badly of them but express yourself positively. Devote yourself to your life's work, with the mindset that asks, "How can I make Buddha happy?"

If you harbor negative thoughts, bad words and bad actions will come from you. If you harbor good thoughts, good words and actions will come. That is why the focus of our spiritual practice should be to cleanse ourselves of *sim-eop* (mental sins). If you think that others are Buddhas and embed this thought in your mind, you will not commit sins.

Just as you must plant merit without committing sins, in order to plant even a little more merit, you must turn yourself to the Heavens and Buddha. If your mindset is to revere the Heavens and serve Buddha, then the work you do for Buddha and for yourself will both be successful. But if your mindset is to look after your own interests first, neither Buddha work nor personal work will go particularly well for you.

THE ESSENCE OF SPIRITUAL PRACTICE

A person who once resided at the monastery used to tell others that he had come in order to plant merit for himself, to further his study, and to awaken his Dharma power. This person did not understand the meaning of spiritual practice.

If you revere the Heavens and serve Buddha, sacrifice and devote yourself to the monastery, then there is no "I" involved because it is all washed away. Cleansing the ego in this way is spiritual practice. When you surrender greed, anger, and arrogance, your wisdom and Dharma power will grow. This is the ultimate goal. Only then will you plant merit and not commit sins.

If you simply enjoy the clean air and water of the monastery, but don't listen to your teacher and cling to your own thoughts, your own ways, and your karmic hindrances, then your stay at the monastery will have little meaning. You must watch closely how you use your mind, what you say, and what you do. If you criticize people with your mind, talk behind someone's back or verbally abuse an advanced practitioner, this is a serious error. A spiritual seeker must be absolutely honest and diligent, and will thus plant much merit. But those who lie, look for excuses, and are dishonest will only plant a small amount of merit. Treating Buddha's wealth as your own is also a grave mistake. Those who cultivate their mind never use the monastery's money for their own purposes.

As you plant merit by farming at the monastery, making meju, and pressing sesame oil, you must lower yourself and be humble—if you show off to others, are boastful or lose your temper, it will not become merit. If you are greedy for merit or lustful, then your work will not become merit either. Your mind has to be free of greed, anger, and arrogance for the wisdom-eye of the mind to open. This is the standard by which spiritual seekers practice and live. Ordinarily, people live as they do because they are ignorant, but advanced practitioners do not live in this way. A teacher who is honest and sincere, who practices virtue and charity and lives according to this path—is he or she not your guide?

STRENGTHS AND WEAKNESSES

You must make a habit of keeping your promises, for this becomes your character and trustworthiness. If you do not keep your word, your conscience weakens, and karmic hindrances will take stronger root.

There is a practitioner who rarely finishes things properly, misleads others and makes excuses. This is because she repeatedly practiced this way for many lives. One practitioner always takes the easiest, most convenient route, again because it has been his habit for many lives. Another practitioner, however, always says "yes" to his teacher's words and follows them faithfully, because this is what he has practiced for many lives.

Everyone has strengths and weaknesses. Making use of one's strengths while correcting one's faults is spiritual practice and study. But people generally do not see themselves clearly. When you are at the monastery, you can recognize your flawed self and be awakened to its true condition. You cannot change what you don't know, but what you do know, you can change. Before I leave this world, you must change, and lay the foundations of spiritual practice in your mind.

In my spiritual practice, if there was something I did not want to do, I recited *Mireukjon Yeoraebul* and worked even harder on that task to overcome the mind of dislike. As that mind was surrendered, I no longer disliked or hated the work.

While also surrendering the mind of liking something, you should not lose yourself in, or be bound to, what you like doing, and so be free. When it comes to planting virtue, what is there to like or dislike? If you only do what you like, and don't do what you dislike, how can you plant virtue?

If you have an aversion to certain tasks, keep surrendering that mind until it is cleansed, and then you will find the task easier. The mind that doesn't want to work is a lazy mind, but if you keep surrendering it, it will be cleansed.

You need to eradicate that mind while I am still here; otherwise, when will you do it? If you don't eradicate it, it will be a heavy burden on you since you will be working with the mind of dislike for many lives to come. All you have to do is simply put these words into practice. If you make a resolution to change, you can change immediately.

SACRIFICE YOUR LIFE TO CULTIVATE THE MIND

I once had a friend who went to a prestigious high school, and was elected the school president. He was highly intelligent, had very pure mind, and was very popular among the female students. However, one day after finishing college, he told me that he had decided to marry the hostess of a seedy drinking house who was six or seven years his senior.

Since he came from a poor family, I hoped that he would marry a woman who was diligent and kindhearted, so it caused me great distress to hear his news. Since I treat others' matters like my own, I was lost for words. I thought that he was going to ruin his life, so I tried to dissuade him. But he said he had already made up his mind, and there was no point in trying to talk to him out of it. His two elder brothers told him he was mad, scolded him and urged him to break off the marriage, but he did not listen to them.

As his lungs were weak, he was in no condition to have an active married life, and in the end he did not live very long. His problem was his weak mind, and he gave in to the woman out of soft-heartedness. Everyone must cleanse the karmic hindrances he or she has practiced for many lives. This is for the sake of your eternal life.

My friend could not join the monastery nor cleanse his mind, and so he died. Think about yourselves—if you do not cultivate the mind even after joining the monastery, what will become of you in your next life? You must have a fierce determination— one that is willing to sacrifice even your own life—to cleanse the mind. Without compromise or exception, when a mind arises, you must curb it with your will, collect yourself and use all your strength to cleanse your mind. Your mentality should be one of offering up your life to do it.

When the karmic hindrances in the mind are cleansed away, evil fortunes and evil destiny will turn to good fortune and a good destiny.

YOUR FELLOW PRACTITIONERS ARE YOUR TEACHERS

If you see that your fellow practitioners are better than you in certain respects, do your best to emulate them and put these points into practice. If you see your fellow practitioner doing something wrong, you should use your fellow practitioner's example as a guide to help you progress, and be sure to avoid doing the same thing. Live your whole life in this way, both inside and outside the monastery.

A fellow practitioner is a teacher and a mirror. Your colleagues teach you what to do and what not to do in your life. Even if you were to base your study on this alone, it would progress considerably.

How grateful you should be to those who stir up quarrels and disturb others, for by sacrificing themselves and dragging themselves downwards they are giving you a lesson. If you do not put such lessons into practice, then there is no meaning or benefit to their actions.

THREE POISONOUS MINDS

When you meet someone who does not practice to purify their greed, anger, or arrogance, it feels uncomfortable for some reason. But when you meet a practitioner who has less greed and anger, who is gentle, modest, and cultivates the mind well, your head feels clear and your mind is at ease. The energy of such practitioners purifies and brightens their surroundings.

You must purify yourself of the three poisonous minds by reining in your materialistic and sensual desires, restraining anger, lowering yourself, and practicing the intent to learn from others. By being considerate towards others, being helpful to them, sacrificing yourself to attend to their needs, you practice the Bodhisattva Mind and the Bodhisattva Act, and thus tread the Bodhisattva Path. This is spiritual practice.

Your mind will become ordered if you keep your room and clothes clean, organize your belongings, air the room frequently, and arrange your shoes in neat order. Set your mind upon practicing the Bodhisattva Mind, practicing the Bodhisattva Act, and following the Bodhisattva Path while, in your daily life, you keep your room clean and your belongings tidy, and keep lowering yourself. Such are the basics of a practitioner's life. Coveting material possessions and seeking sensual pleasures, giving way to anger, and being arrogant—this is a foolish way to live.

When the weather is warmer and I am able to visit Pohang again for Dharma meetings, I will do a spot check of practitioners' rooms. It is because I hold you dear that I look to every aspect of your practice and keep pressuring you so that you can change.

CHANGE AT ONCE

Before she became a practitioner, Y was pale and unwell because she had lived on snacks and noodles, and rarely had a proper meal. She changed her diet after joining the monastery, and now she looks better and is healthy again. Practitioner K was unwell because of her unbalanced diet, eating only the rice and side-dishes she liked, even when at the monastery. Y changed immediately, but K did not, because she is unwise.

A doctor of traditional Asian medicine once told me that if you don't eat well for just two weeks, you will suffer the effects in full when you reach old age—for this is how sensitive the body is to one's diet. Through poor eating habits, people ruin the body of their future. Thinking it was acceptable to do so, the practitioner insisted on her unhealthy eating habits, but her thoughts were not correct. Eating poorly ruins the body of one lifetime, and a wrong mindset ruins one's eternity.

It is the mark of an unwise person to live stubbornly according to their own thoughts. Wise people strive to change themselves following the teachings of Buddha, of living saints, and of their teacher.

Some practitioners try to correct their shortcomings, but others do not. You must ceaselessly devote your utmost efforts to changing yourself.

When a person who follows the spiritual path guides you, you need to change right away. If you do things your own way, there will be no progress. Because people live in ignorance and darkness, they make mistakes and encounter failure in everything they do. You can only change when you realize that you are lacking, and when you try to learn from others. But because you are unaware of this, I keep telling you so that you can realize it. When a person who treads the spiritual path points out a flaw in you, change it right away. You must change at once—your mind, habits and actions, once and for all.

KEEP BUDDHA IN YOUR MIND

Those who cultivate the mind well never take a life, practice deception, or commit sin. Living honestly, they strive for perfection in their work, and their lives are always guided by asking "Will Buddha like this or not?" So, practice giving, perform good deeds, and plant virtue whenever you can. What else is there you must do?

Even if all twenty-four hours of the day are spent in spiritual practice and working at the monastery, the mind will be cultivated and your efforts will become great merit only when there is Buddha in your mind. On the other hand, if there is no Buddha, the mind will not be cultivated and your efforts will not become great merit. In a mind where there is no Buddha, there is only room for karmic hindrance. The ego and karmic hindrances will take their place in the mind, and carry out the deeds of karmic hindrances. You do not recite *Mireukjon Yeoraebul* to the empty air, but to your mind. Each and everyday, you must surrender what is within your mind by reciting *Mireukjon Yeoraebul* to it, and awaken to realizations.

Cleansing your karmic hindrances, preconceptions, and flaws is spiritual practice. It is a grave error indeed if, content with your present circumstances, you live without the will to cultivate the mind and become like Buddha. In order to become like Buddha, you must lower yourself, hold others in high esteem, and respect. You must generate the intention to learn from them in order for your study to progress. You need to cultivate your own mind—you cannot cultivate someone else's. The moment you hear this, practice it immediately on the spot.

I am happiest when you study well and awaken to realizations. At that moment, I feel the joy of having taken care of you. Do not disappoint me by being unmindful, and do not cause me anxiety by doing bad deeds. I hope with all my heart that you will bring me more such joy by achieving realizations and by putting these realizations into practice.

SIN-EON-SEO-PAN: BODY, WORDS, WRITING AND DECISION

When selecting government officials, or prospective sons-in-law or daughters-in-law, the character and qualities of an individual have traditionally been judged with reference to the four standards—*Sin-eon-seo-pan*. *Sin* refers to countenance, presence, and conduct; *eon* refers to ways of speech; *seo* refers to writing; and *pan* refers to decision-making.

Since a face is the window to a person's mind, the mind has to be cultivated well for the face to be warm, gentle, and relaxed. If the mind is ordered, one's conduct will be orderly as well. Words and speech must be logical without causing upset to others. The level of education and character can be discerned from writing, and decision-making abilities are important because the success and failure of one's livelihood depend upon it.

Thinking on this, how should you change, and what should you develop?

AS IF THIS DAY WERE YOUR LAST

I heard that Tibetan monks, before going to bed every night, tidy and arrange their bowls and belongings as if preparing for death. No one knows which will come first—the next day or the next life. In this way, practitioners should cultivate their mind and plant merit, thinking that today is the last day of their life.

If today were the last day, few people could confidently say that they had led a good life. As you look back on your life, atone and repent for your wrongful acts. Since today is the last day of this life, you should be planting virtue with every act and with every thought, without missing a moment. You should practice the mentality of serving Buddha with reverence, and practice the bright and devout mind.

Face everyone with the belief that he or she is precious and worthier than yourself, and regard others with the mindset of finding out what you can learn from them.

You must live for Buddha; you must devote and dedicate yourself for the benefit of many people and your surroundings. Never hurt another's feelings, nor cause them physical harm. Live your life carefully like this, and you will commit less sin and plant merit.

You must live in great vigilance, stemming from a belief that today is the last day of your life. Then your study will progress.

PRACTITIONER

To think "I have studied for a long time" because you joined the monastery before others—is a thought to be ashamed of. Such a person cannot be called a practitioner, or one who purifies the mind. If you cannot surrender and subdue your greed, personal interest, or desire for fame, how can you say you are a practitioner?

Someone who is humble and lowers himself before others, who reveres and looks up to the Heavens and Buddha, who devotes himself to the monastery and his country, and who follows the Bodhisattva Path while practicing the Bodhisattva Mind and Bodhisattva Acts—such a person can be called a practitioner. Devoting and sacrificing your life for the benefit of many people is following the Bodhisattva Path. You must live your eternity like this.

This is how I have tried to live every single moment of my life. I have lived with those of you present here nineteen, or twenty-four years, but even when I set the example, one or two out of the twenty-four people do not follow well. As you breathe the pure air, drink the clean water, and eat the wholesome foods that we produce—even as you enjoy such privileges, if you do not have the mind of a bodhisattva or practice the deeds of a bodhisattva, how can you be called a practitioner? You are no different from a person who does not cultivate the mind. In spite of the privileges you receive, are you not falling short in your study?

Because I hold you dear, I do my best, and come and speak to you even as I exercise. But I wonder whether one or two of you are doing your best simply to protect your status and put yourself forward.

THE METHOD OF PRACTICE

The mind of greed, anger, and arrogance—to study means to purify these three things.

At the very moment when you see something and want to possess it, you should not lose your chance, but recite *Mireukjon Yeoraebul* to that mind straightaway to calm your greed. This is spiritual practice. Surrendering lust the moment it arises, this too is spiritual practice. When anger, irritation, and hate arise, reciting *Mireukjon Yeoraebul* on those minds to calm them is practice, and when you feel proud or boastful, reciting *Mireukjon Yeoraebul* on these minds for ten, twenty, or thirty minutes until they disappear is practice. Surrendering the mind at the very moment it arises, without letting it slip away, is practice.

We cannot be freed from our karmic hindrances if they do not surface from the depths of the mind. When they arise, do not be troubled, or think to yourself "Why must I endure this arising mind again?" but recite *Mireukjon Yeoraebul* to it intensely, and it will melt away.

That mind that arises is our mind, our wealth, and what we have practiced for countless lives. One's house or the property is the wealth of one lifetime, but what we must ultimately deal with is the inner wealth that we possess—the three poisons and the karmic hindrances in our mind, which we have carried with us for so many lives in the past, and which we will carry forward with us for countless lives in the future.

We read the Diamond Sutra in the morning and evening, and recite *Mireukjon Yeoraebul* throughout the day to increase our power of surrendering. Thus, when a karmic hindrance arises, we can surrender it and not be deceived. When a karmic hindrance arises, surrender it devotedly and with reverence to Buddha, and it will melt away like ice under the sun. The person who does this is a wise student.

You must surrender karmic hindrances as they arise. If you miss the moment, they will fall back into your mind, and you will have missed the opportunity to be freed from them.

Read and recite the Diamond Sutra on your flaws and your karmic hindrances, and always watch your mind. Whether it arises faintly or fiercely, if you recite *Mireukjon Yeoraebul* to it, you will be liberated.

WHEN YOU DO MONASTERY WORK

When you do monastery work, you should turn yourself to Buddha. Do not work half-heartedly or absent-mindedly, but with the mindset of contributing to the monastery. Do your job thoroughly and pay attention to detail, consult knowledgeable people to find the best method, and give your utmost effort. You may say that I am strict and pedantic. But, as you turn to the Heavens and work for Buddha, if you don't work like this, you are making a mistake.

If personal motives or karmic hindrances get in the way, you cannot walk the path to enlightenment. How could your practice progress when you are deceiving the Heavens, deceiving Buddha, and betraying your conscience? Whether or not someone is watching, doing your utmost is the Dharma of Buddha. When you work like this, you will plant much merit, and through that virtue, your wisdom-eye will open. One whose wisdom-eye has been opened is an enlightened master.

THE PATH OF THE BODHISATTVA

A great part of Buddha's teaching is concerned with how to cultivate and purify the mind while living for the benefit of others. The teaching of Dangun (the ruler who founded Korea in 2333 BC), which states that our life should bring great benefit to mankind, is similar in spirit.

Repenting and lowering ourselves, while cultivating and retaining control of our inner world, embracing the Bodhisattva Mind, and practicing the Bodhisattva Act, is Buddhism. The mindset of Buddha and the bodhisattvas is one of compassion and of benefitting others.

Among the practitioners, there are some who quietly devote themselves to working for Buddha and the monastery without idleness or excuse, and practice humility. They pick up the work gloves scattered here and there in the monastery grounds, remove the litter left behind by others, and make repairs around the monastery where they are needed. The Buddha and bodhisattvas take delight in such people.

The Diamond Sutra states "The Tathagata perceives the mind of every sentient being in every corner of the universe." This means that Buddha sees everything that moves deep in the minds of sentient beings at each moment. Before bright wisdom, there is no place to hide. This is why those who quietly dedicate themselves to hard work without trying to impress me or senior practitioners plant the greatest merit. Buddha dislikes those who try to show off or boast about themselves, bully others, or enjoy asserting their authority. Depending on the kind of mindset you have in planting merit, the level of merit you accumulate will be different. How then could you fail to do your best when planting merit, and how could you not lower yourself and cultivate the mind? It could be said that someone who works this way practices the mindset of an owner. Carefully looking after the monastery with the mindset of an owner means to work for the benefit and comfort of those around you. This is the Bodhisattva Act, and comes from putting the Bodhisattva Mind into practice.

By quietly devoting yourself to the monastery's work, practicing the mindset of an owner and becoming the healthy owner of your own mind, and practicing the Bodhisattva Mind that serves with constant dedication as a member of the Diamond Sutra Recitation Group, you will step forward into the world of bright virtue. To practice the Bodhisattva Mind and Bodhissatva Act is to follow the Boddhisttva Path.

PREPARING THE MONASTERIES

In 1973, after seven years and six months at Sosa Monastery, Master Kim established the Diamond Sutra Recitation Group in his hometown of Pohang at the age of thirty-three. Today, he is the head of a group of fifteen monasteries and Dharma halls in Korea, the United States, the United Kingdom, and Germany, including the two monasteries where full-time practitioners reside. Until a few years ago, he never spoke of the difficulties and hardships he had to face while establishing the monasteries and Dharma halls. Then, one day, he told us the following story, saying that he hoped knowing these things would help our practice.

When I was young, I started a small business to support my sister's education, and sent her abroad to study in West Germany. After she became a nurse, she told me to join her in Germany, saying that it was now her turn to support me. This was after I had resolved to devote myself to spiritual practice, however, so I told her that I would stay in Korea. When she heard this, she sent me all the money she had saved. The salary of a nurse in Germany at the time was eight or nine times more than that of a civil servant in Korea: if a Korean civil servant earned ten dollars, a nurse in Germany received eighty, ninety dollars. Because she only spent her money on necessities, she had saved a lot of money. With this money, I built three stores and a small Dharma hall at Uhyeon-dong in Pohang. I also built a small house at Sinheung-dong where my mother could live.

To save money when building the Dharma hall, I hired only those laborers that I absolutely needed, and took part in the building myself, working harder than they did. Because it was expensive to buy brick, I used four-inch perforated blocks of cement instead.

The walls were six centimeters thick, the ceiling was made of thin plywood, and the roof was slate. When the winter came, the wind would whistle through the gaps, and because I lived using only a single coal briquette per day, the room was freezing at night. I covered my face with a blanket, and because my head was cold, I took out my winter coat and covered my head with it.

One day, Mr. Yang Chan-yeong, who had come down from Seoul to Daegu for some building work, stopped by to insulate the Dharma hall. Instead of insulating with polystyrene like today, he filled the gap with a machine-generated foam. He did this to fill the Dharma hall with warmth. His reverence and devotion were great, and my heart was deeply touched. His wife has been preparing meals at the Youth Dharma meetings in Seoul and paying for the food with her own money for twenty four years now. I know of no one else like them.

Eventually, an apartment complex was built behind the Dharma hall at Uhyeondong. To make the neighborhood look tidier, construction managers from the apartment complex visited and offered to convert the twenty-seven square-meter study room into a two-storey house at no charge. Once the conversion started, however, it would take several months to finish, and the eight lay followers who came to study at the Dharma hall every morning would no longer be able to attend. I was worried that if their morning practice stopped for several months, they would end their practice altogether and would be unable to cultivate their minds in this lifetime. I also felt reluctant to have the walls knocked down, barely a year after Mr. Yang's efforts had made the room so warm.

The construction team visited me four times, but I could never bring myself to do it as my mind was never comfortable with the idea. It would of course have been to my benefit if they had built a two-storey house free of charge. They were professional apartment builders and would have done a fine job. But if the Dharma hall had disappeared for five months, it seemed to me that the lay followers would abandon their study as their good roots were not very deep. They had waited and waited for countless lives to come and visit me, and my conscience would not allow me to proceed. So I gave up on the idea of having a two-storey house built.

To save money on coal briquettes, I cooked all the rice in the morning needed for breakfast and lunch, which were the two meals I had each day. I had no side dishes, and when making soup, I added some soybean paste to faucet water. In winter I added bean sprouts and soybean paste to the water, and in summer I added spinach and soybean paste. I made soups using just three ingredients. Some chili pepper powder or sesame oil should have been added to make it more nutritious, but I couldn't afford those. Rice and soup were all I could eat. Besides, in the belief that a spiritual practitioner should not overeat, I lived on just enough food to stave off hunger. At that time, what I really longed to eat was kimchi. However, after first offering the meals up to Buddha with gratitude, I ate in happiness without any sense of lack.

This is how I lived for the first three years of my ten-year stay at Uhyeon-dong. For the next four years, as I had begun to receive a little more rent, I was able to add kimchi and *dubu* [Korean tofu] to the meal, and so I cooked and ate this way for seven years. Even as I was eating in this manner, I still read the Diamond Sutra seven times every morning from 4 A.M., kept the evening study times, visited other monasteries to give Dharma lectures, and travelled across the country for the Memorial Day services. My nose bled frequently from fatigue and malnutrition, and when I sat down or got up, the whole sky appeared to be yellow, and I saw flashes of light and felt dizzy. Since I was unable to continue this way any longer, during the last three years at Uhyeon-dong, I ate two meals at a cheap restaurant. It is said that if you don't eat properly for just a fortnight, you will feel all the adverse effects in your old age. Because of the hard manual labor I did for seven years at Sosa, and because I ate so poorly for seven years at Uhyeon, I am very sensitive to the cold today, to the extent that I cannot even go outside in winter.

The layout of the Uhyeon-dong Dharma hall was such that one entered the Dharma hall through the kitchen, and as the lay followers came and went throughout the day for their study, they would open my pots and the cabinets in the kitchen, wondering what Master Kim was eating.

The Uhyeon Dharma hall was located in the downtown area, and it occurred to me that a Dharma hall at the foot of a quiet, peaceful mountain would help people's practice more. So I altered the terms of the store's lease, which had been generating a monthly rent, and received a lump-sum payment. With that money, I bought a plot of land on which to build another Dharma hall for the lay followers, a little further from Uhyeon and at the foot of a mountain. Later, the price of the land rose considerably, and I was able to sell it to buy the twenty six acres of land in the mountain area where the Gyeongju Monastery is today.

The Diamond Monastery was also built with much difficulty. In the case of the other monasteries in each region, half the funding was provided centrally, and the rest was donated by lay followers who each gave a little as part of the Buddha work to support their own monasteries. The lay followers who came to the monastery received the grace of Buddha. In one case, a person whose business was on the point of closing down managed to save it after offering up prayers, and in gratitude donated money for Buddha work.

This is how the eight monasteries were established. They are not in my name, but owned by a non-profit entity whose bylaws provide that, when the Diamond Sutra Recitation Group dissolves, all its assets will revert to the state. I possess nothing as my own. The house at Sinheung where my mother used to live was sold and the proceeds offered up to Buddha. I also sold the Uhyeon-dong Dharma hall in the downtown area, and used the money to purchase the Chogok monastery in the suburbs. The difference in price I offered up to Buddha. This is the path of a practitioner—living without hint of reproach.

Before the current monastery at Seongbuk in Seoul existed, the Seoul monastery was at Hyehwa. When we were no longer allowed to use the monastery at Hyehwa, I felt in my heart like a parent who had been cast out with his children, with nowhere to go but the streets. Even if the monastery in Seoul were to close down, I still had a place to stay in Pohang, the Diamond Monastery, the Gyeongju Monastery, and the other monasteries in Ulsan, Daegu, and Busan. But if the Seoul monastery disappeared, the lay followers there would not be able to plant merit or cultivate and brighten their minds. As I cared for them like my own family, I was devastated that their next lives might become difficult as a result. It brought tears to my eyes, as if it was happening to me. It pained my heart to think that a traveler on his way to a bright eternity might turn his back on the path to Buddha, and fall instead into darkness.

The cost to build the monastery at Seongbuk was just under a million dollars. The headquarters provided three hundred thousand, which came from selling traditional foods, our clothing store, and donations from the regional monasteries. Among the members of the Seoul monastery at that time, some were well off and others were not, but we collected a flat membership fee of ten dollars every month for the new monastery fund, which after five years amounted to two hundred and fifty thousand dollars. We began collecting ten dollars a month in the very first month of the Hyehwa monastery's opening, in case the landlords decided to sell off the premises. When they heard that the Hyehwa Monastery had been sold, the lay followers came together and contributed the remaining two hundred and fifty thousand. The cost of renovating the newly purchased Seoul monastery came to fifty thousand dollars, and to minimize cost, the practitioners went to Seoul to do the repairs themselves. To run monasteries and temples without wearing a monk's robe or shaving one's head—this was unheard of at the time, forty or fifty years ago.

I mention these stories from the past so that at least you—the practitioners—will revere the Heavens, revere Buddha, and endeavor to care for the Diamond Sutra Recitation Group, and live a life of cultivating the mind and planting merit. This is all I could ask of you.

S i x t e e n

Practice in Daily Life

This chapter contains stories about
Master Kim told by his students.
The anecdotes have been written by many
different practitioners, and accordingly
the viewpoint of "I" differs throughout.

There is a famous dialogue between Master Dao Lin and Scholar Bai Le Tian with which every Buddhist is familiar.

"Master Dao Lin, what is the great truth of Buddha Dharma?"

"It is to not commit bad deeds while diligently performing good deeds."

"But that is something even a three-year-old knows, is it not?"

"It is something that a three-year old might know, but that even an eighty-year old finds difficult to do."

There are many noble words and teachings in the world but, as the tale illustrates, putting them into practice is the difficult part. Also, it shows that the problem is one of application and practice, not knowledge.

At our monastery, practitioners have lived under the guidance of Master Kim for as long as twenty four years in some cases, and as short as five years in others. He never gives us instructions without practicing them himself, and seeing how his words are always consistent with his actions, we have come to deeply revere our master.

A lay follower once said, "When you peel away at someone like peeling an onion, you often see that their inside and outside are different, and that their inside is darker than the outside. But when the master shows his inside, even just a little, it is the inside that is brighter and cleaner, so my head naturally bows down in humility." It is as if she was voicing our minds, and we understand exactly what she means.

By studying under Master Kim, we have come to understand,

little by little, the spiritual level of Confucius and what he meant when he said "at the age of seventy, even when I did as I wanted, I transgressed neither the laws nor morality." For countless lives, because his sole purpose in life has been to revere and serve Buddha, and because he has constantly walked the Bodhisattva Path, even his casual acts or informal words are in perfect unison with the Dharma, and there is always something that awakens us to the Truth.

By seeing how he lives, we have come to comprehend what is truly meant by virtues such as kindness, devotion, self-restraint, compassion, love, and reverence—virtues which we had hitherto only understood as an abstract concept, and we pledge to practice them ourselves. Though it is difficult for us to fathom his bright world that is both deep and vast, in our humble measure, we have set out below what we have seen, heard, and felt while studying under Master Kim, predominantly in the form of anecdotes.

I SHOULD DO MY OWN CHORES

Until the age of seventy, Master Kim always did his own laundry and cleaning. Every morning and evening, he wiped his room with a wet cloth, and hand-washed his clothes rather than use a washing machine. When we told him that we would do his laundry and cleaning, he would always reply, "I should do my own chores" and did them himself. Then when he turned seventy, because of the pain in his back and knees, he delegated the task of cleaning the room to us and began to use a washing machine, though he still hand-washes small items such as underwear and socks.

When he does his laundry, he uses a tiny amount of detergent powder—no more than the size of a small bean—and soaks his clothes in a basin of water. To make sure that the detergent does not pollute the river, he pours away the dirty water in the yard and never down the washroom drain. It must be tiresome to dispose of the detergent water like this every time, but this is what he always does.

When we make fruit juice and offer it up in a bottle, he always washes the bottle personally before giving it back to us. Even when we say that we will wash it for him, he invariably rinses it clean and hands it back to us.

As we attend Master Kim, we realize that the teachings contained in his writings or Dharma lectures are not a mere theory he developed to help our spiritual study, but they simply represent the reality of how he lived and how he practiced. It is the same with his teaching about not craving things from others

328

but taking care of one's own tasks and looking after others. While walking in the mountains, if he sees a long piece of rope or a tree branch on the road, he clears it away in case people think that it is a snake and are startled.

There is a small stone bridge in the monastery. One day, as he went underneath with a practitioner to inspect the flow of water, he cut his hand slightly on a protruding nail. He then began to hammer in the nail with a big, nearby stone until it had completely gone in.

"Why does he do this, when people rarely come here, and no one else will ever set hand on that part of the bridge?" As the practitioner wondered thus, Master Kim explained, "If anyone ever puts their hand here, I want to make sure that they won't be hurt."

To the young practitioner, the sound of Master Kim hammering the nail came as a teaching that, like this, one who cleanses the "I" must always care for and look after others at any moment, and it echoed deep in her heart.

PUTTING OTHERS FIRST

Until the early 1990s, we used coal-briquette boilers at the Diamond Monastery. Coal boilers had become something of a rarity by then as the national economy had much improved, but we only changed over to the new oil boilers at the start of the 1990s. We couldn't make the change in one go either, and replaced the boilers one by one, as and when we could afford it. The boiler at the female quarters was changed first, and then the male quarters, and finally Master Kim's own room was changed last. We repeatedly recommended that the master should change his first, but he adamantly declined.

None of the buildings at the Diamond Monastery were built by construction companies or by external engineers. They have all been built by Master Kim, his practitioners, and the lay followers. Around ten years ago, the master suggested that the practitioners' sleeping quarters be converted into mud houses for the benefit of our health. Like he did with the boilers, he changed the female rooms first and then the male rooms, but this time he did not make a mudroom for himself. Ashamed that only we were sleeping inside the healthy mud houses, we sought his permission on many occasions to build him a mudroom, but he declined each time saying, "There's no need since I am old, and it will soon be time for me to leave." It was only five years after our mudrooms had been built that he finally gave us permission to build him the same.

Living under the guidance of a master who always puts and thinks of others first, we often feel grateful and ashamed at the

same time, for it seems that we are being served by him rather
than us serving the master.

PUTTING THE MONASTERY FIRST

Just as he always thinks of others first, even if there is something urgent or inconvenient, the master always waits and defers to the monastery work schedule.

The busiest period at the monastery is early winter when meju (fermented soybean block) is made. At the end of December, after we had finished making meju, the master gave me a call. He inquired about the monastery work and which tasks kept us busy. When I explained that we had a little spare time as meju-making had finished, he asked if I could cut the branches of a chestnut tree standing in front of his room.

Because the master is very sensitive to the cold, he cannot leave his room in winter and, from 11 to 12 in the morning, he bathes in the sunlight coming through the window. But because the chestnut tree had concealed all the light, he could scarcely do this, and would have been greatly inconvenienced by the darkness of the room. Yet, he had waited until the Buddha work of making meju had finished before giving me a call.

WHY WE MUST BE FRUGAL

Master Kim is remarkably organized in his daily life, and he is very strict when it comes to being frugal. His room is clean and tidy, his shoes are always neatly arranged, and he frequently airs his bedding and clothes in the sun.

He wears an undershirt until it has twenty holes or more, and he sews up any holes in his socks or outer garments. But because the thread in his possession does not come in different colors but only in brown, Master Kim's shirts, pants, and socks all have patches of brown.

He wore the same pair of sneakers at the monastery for nearly ten years until the soles became so tattered that his socks showed right through. As for the shoes he wears to Dharma Lectures, he has been wearing the same pair for sixteen years after replacing the heels that had worn out once. He never uses an entire sheet of facial tissue, always dividing it into two or four pieces, and he uses his wiping cloth until it has split into so many strands that I sometimes wonder if it is actually possible to clean the room with it.

Even though he acutely feels the cold, he keeps his room cool during wintertime to save the boiler oil, and he stays indoors wearing a hat, a mask, and thick clothing.

At the monastery, we use the surface water from the mountains to do our laundry, washing-up, shower, and other daily tasks, and we use the groundwater for drinking. Once a day, we put the groundwater in a glass bottle and offer it up to our master. One day, as we offered up the fresh water and took away the bottle from the previous day, our master asked what we were going to do with the old water left in the bottle. Because it would be wasted if we simply threw it away, he told us to use it for washing dishes. After a meal, if there is any soybean paste or soy sauce left, however little there is, he tells us to re-use it when cooking his soup.

In the winter before last, the pain in his back, hips, and knee joints became severe and he found it difficult to even sit or stand. One of the practitioners went into his room and filled the kettle with water to warm his medicine but, even amid the pain, the master worried that the practitioner would waste water and electricity, and told him to use the minimum amount of water as boiling a large quantity uses lots of electricity.

But when the practitioner threw away the water left in the kettle into the bathroom floor drain without much thought, the master scolded him, saying that he could have used it to wash his feet in the evening if he had poured it into the basin instead, adding "Even though we do not pay any water bills because we use the groundwater and the surface water from the mountains, but we must still conserve and save what the Heavens have given us." I have often heard the master speak similar words at Dharma lectures, but seeing him meticulously put them into practice in his daily life made them sound much more solemn.

One day, a crack appeared in the plastic basin that our master uses in the bathroom, so he asked us to buy a new one from the market. However, nothing at the market was exactly the same size, and there were only basins that were slightly bigger or slightly smaller. Rather than buy something that was too small, we thought that the master would find it easier to do his laundry in a bigger basin, so we bought and offered up the larger one. But the master said that a large basin leads to wasting water, so he made us go back and exchange it for the smaller one.

Usually, people look after their own belongings because they were purchased with their own money, but they are often wasteful and careless with public facilities or communal properties. At home, people might save on water to reduce their water bill but, at public bathhouses, after paying the entrance fee, some use the water extravagantly, and expend it literally like the phrase "spending money like water." While they keep their homes clean, people carelessly litter in the mountains or the seaside. Indeed, some even mistakenly believe that doing so means having a good time. As our master impresses upon us, paying for something doesn't mean it belongs to us. Rather, we are simply borrowing it for a short period that has been bestowed upon us by the Heavens and, unless we save and are grateful for its use, our merit will all leak out. This is why he teaches us to save and use public property with care as if it were our own.

Several years ago, the local authorities paved the road from the village to the monastery, and the roadwork managers told us that we could drive over it after a day since the paving hardens overnight. But our master said, "It only hardens completely after three days. It's all state property, so you must treat it with care so that it lasts for a long time," and forbade us from driving over the pavement for three days.

Not so long ago, a lay-follower living nearby suggested contacting the local authorities to install streetlights along the roads to the monastery, noting how inconvenient it must be for us to have the roads unlit at night. But given that there is very little traffic to and from the monastery at night, and the roads can be seen adequately from the vehicle headlights alone, our master declined, noting that while her thoughts were kind, one must be careful when spending the nation's wealth.

The master's extremely frugal ways and spirit that underlies his actions, it seems to me, are teachings of great compassion that awaken us to how we must live as practitioners. One day, the master wrapped a few undershirts riddled with holes into a plastic bag, gave them to a practitioner, and asked him to burn them in the incinerator. The practitioner took the bag away, put it in the miniature incinerator and left to run other errands, intending to burn it at night. But several hours later, the master asked if he had burnt the undershirts yet, adding that if he hadn't, he should keep a couple of the shirts.

"When I'm gone, I hope people will save and be thrifty when they see these shirts. Apparently there are no wells in some regions in Africa so people have to drink the dirty water. With the money they save by being frugal, I hope people will help and build wells for those people living in such hardship."

On hearing these words, I felt humbled no end. His words encouraging us to repay even a little of the limitless love received from Buddha, by being grateful for the grace of the Heavens, by saving and treating things with care, and by using less for myself while giving more to others—I vow to never forget these words, and pledge to practice them for all incarnations.

YOUR EVERYDAY LIFE MUST CHANGE

Master Kim stresses that the cultivation of the mind is not something that naturally comes about by spending a long time at a monastery. It is done by identifying and correcting, one by one, the bad habits and negative mindsets that we practice in our daily lives.

He once scolded a practitioner severely on seeing her walk with her shoes crumpled down at the back, saying that "to crumple your shoes is to crumple your mind." He dislikes it when we wear clothes that are off-season, or when we leave our buttons undone, or when we drag the tips of our pants along the ground. He ensures that our clothes are modest, appropriate for the weather and the season, and are clean and tidy at the same time.

In his Dharma lectures, he frequently tells us good habits which we can practice in everyday life. Stressing that people who cultivate their mind must consider and yield to others, when we park our car, he tells us to park right up to the wall, barely five to ten centimeters away, so that we do not inconvenience the other drivers. When we sound the horn, because we will startle and disturb the nearby drivers or pedestrians if we sound long and hard, he tells us to press the horn lightly and for no more than a few seconds.

When we give advice to someone, he also explains that it must be borne out of concern and care for that person. With family members or close friends, we often point out their faults right away on the spot. But since this is likely to hurt their feelings, he

337

notes that the way of spiritual seekers is to wait until the other person is calm enough to accept your advice, and then admonish with positive and soft words. And he teaches us to speak with a sincere mind that pleases the others' mind, and not their ears.

WHAT ARE YOUR THOUGHTS

Master Kim is someone who is very free in asking questions and seeking the opinions of others, whenever and wherever. Despite being the most senior person at the monastery, the phrase we hear most frequently from him is "What do you think?" Always lending his ears to what people have to say, he looks for things to learn.

Before coming to a decision, he always asks the experts in the field, listens and learns from their practical experience, and gathers as much information as possible. He then analyzes the question in detail, reviews it from multiple angles, and comes to the optimal conclusion.

The following happened one summer when the crops were wilting in the scorching drought. Because we do not have any irrigation facilities at the monastery, and rely solely on storing the water flowing down from the mountain valleys to farm our two-and-a-half acres of land, farming becomes difficult in times of drought. Unable to do anything but watch the crops burn dry, we too burned with anxiety when our master called us before him one day.

There is a small pool of water by the master's residence and, pointing out how the water was steadily flowing into the drainage, he said, "I think we should make a cement inlet around here in the drain, and store the water to irrigate. What do you think?"

He then took us to an erosion control facility in the neighboring mountain slightly distant from the monastery. Water was flowing a little here too and, giving us the same explanation as before, he said, "I think we should do this to irrigate, what do you think?" and asked us in earnest as if seeking our permission.

Given his wisdom and years of experience, I thought that it was illogical to seek advice from us—young practitioners who had no experience in farming. But I came to realize that constantly lowering himself while seeking the advice and permission of others is how he always uses and keeps his mind – his housekeeping of the mind. Always humble, there is never a time when he gives someone or something less than his full attention. Always taking a close, detailed look while lending both his ears, he learns and takes in information, and having considered all aspects, he gives us comprehensive words of wisdom.

METICULOUS CARE

For the past seventeen years, Master Kim has never left the monastery except to give Dharma lectures, and for the past ten years, he has entrusted the task of checking our progress to the most senior practitioner, devoting himself to spiritual practice and rarely leaving his abode. Even so, he telephones the most senior practitioner on a daily basis to inquire after every member of the monastery family. He cares not just for the practitioners, but even the dogs and cats that we keep.

Before joining the monastery, the practitioner in charge of the kitchen had a bad habit of eating only what she liked. When the master heard that she was still being picky with her food at the monastery, worried that she was not taking in sufficient nutrition, he asked the most senior practitioner to ensure that she had a spoonful of sesame oil and perilla oil every day. "I run sesame and perilla oil factories (referring to how the monastery makes sesame and perilla oil to be self-sufficient), so how could I not feed my own practitioners sesame and perilla oil? If she's tired from preparing the side-dishes, tell her to reduce the number of my side-dishes by a couple."

Once on Teacher's Day, we pulled together our allowance money and offered up a new pair of pants and underwear to our master. As he received the clothing, he again gave us words of wisdom. "Dust and germs get stuck to the clothes in their manufacture and distribution, so it's always hygienic to wash new clothes first. I never wear new clothes without washing them first, so make sure you do the same." Each time I see that mindset of his—never letting a moment slip by, and always remembering to give words of advice for our benefit—my head and mind naturally bow down.

At the monastery, there is a dog named "*Gong-gyeong*" (*lit.* "one who reveres") and a cat called "*Sibong*" (*lit.* "one who serves"). He always asks us to wash their bowls clean before feeding them and, in the summer, he reminds us to never leave their food out for too long because it goes bad easily, and throw away the food and feed them afresh if it has been left out for several hours.

When Gong-gyeong gave birth, we prepared puppy meals with powdered milk once in the morning, and fed them twice a day. When he learned of this, our master remarked that because powdered milk is nutritious, the feed spoils easily, and that the puppies might fall sick if we gave them for lunch what we prepared in the morning. So he asked us to prepare their meal each time, and to serve it in a clean plate. He also mentioned that when he was looking after the calves at the Sosa Monastery, he always wiped their mouths clean with a wet towel after every feed as their mouths otherwise became sore. He asked us to do the same with the puppies by wiping their mouths clean after each milk feed.

About a month after birth, the puppies began to venture outside, and played and napped on the stone-pavement near the practitioners' dormitory. It was early October then and, noting that it was not good for the puppies to nap with their stomach on the cold pavement, the master asked us to lay cardboard and cloth on the floor for them. Thanks to the master's meticulous and compassionate care, the puppies never once fell ill, and grew in good health.

SAFETY COMES FIRST

Master Kim is always concerned about safety and, to me, his mind feels like that of a mother carefully watching her young child play by a river.

In the winter of 2010, due to a heavy blizzard on the East Coast of the United States, events which had been planned to promote awareness of Korea[1] were all cancelled. When he heard this, the master asked me to tell members of the New York Monastery to wear shoes with sufficient grip so that they would not slip while walking on snow or ice. Several hours later, he contacted me again, saying that he forgot to mention something the last time, adding "As you walk on snow or ice, you will hurt your head if you walk with your hands in your pockets and fall. Don't put your hands in your pockets, wear gloves and keep your balance, and this way you will not hurt your head. You can fix a broken arm or a leg, but if you damage your brain, it is an extremely serious issue. Be sure to pass this message on too."

In the summer of 2011, members of "Korea Connection," a French fan club of *Hallyu* (the popular culture of Korea), visited Korea for two weeks. It was decided that the members of the Diamond Sutra Recitation Group would greet them in the traditional dress of *Hanbok* and treat them to traditional Korean cuisine, and the director of the museum in the Bukchon

---

[1] Promoting awareness of Korean culture, ancient and modern, is a key project of Master Kim. As of July 2013, the Diamond Sutra Recitation Group has printed seven hundred thousand books and screened documentary movies to over one hundred thousand people as part of the project. The materials can be found at www.kscpp.net.

Traditional Folk Village kindly let us use the venue free of charge. Seeing that the view was best from the top, the bosallims decided to set the tables on the rooftop. But when he learned of the plan, the master said that as the bosallims went up and down the stairs in their long, traditional dresses, they could seriously injure themselves by tripping on them, so he told them to set the tables on the first floor instead, and prioritize safety over the view. Noting that safety was most important, he said that "We've never had any serious accidents in the forty years that I have been running the Diamond Sutra Recitation Group, and this is because of the grace of Buddha first of all, and secondly because in every task, we put safety first and took care of any issue right away, without any delay, meticulously."

In the winter of 2011, after taking their college entrance exam, two sons of a bosallim who diligently helps with the promotion of Korean culture, briefly came to the Diamond Monastery to take part in the Buddha work of making meju. Even though the monastery is extremely busy when making meju, our master asked the kitchen practitioner to teach the two children how to cook, saying how wonderful it would be if they could make their own food or even prepare meals for their mother when she returned home late after her presentations. He made sure that they were taught how to make basic soups and simple side-dishes, and even to close the valve at the gas pipes after finishing with the stove.

Never harming any living being is the first precept in Buddhism. The Saddharma-smrty-upasthana Sutra explains the cardinal principle as follows.

> So how does one not take a life? If a person sees ants, worms, silkworm moths, toads, grass bugs, or other insects while walking on the road, he then stays clear and takes the longer route, for he protects sentient beings with compassion. Believing in karma and its retribution, he knows the deeds that err in the cycle of birth and death, and wisely observes the law of arising and ceasing. This is called abstinence from taking a life.

Master Kim's absolute adherence to the precept of never harming a life is an invaluable lesson for us to lead a bright life. It was the day that a Dharma meeting was held at the Diamond Monastery. The master was walking the temple grounds when, in great surprise, he hurriedly took a few steps back. Thinking that perhaps a snake had appeared, the practitioner who was attending upon him frantically gazed around, and saw before them a small earthworm crawl past. It was a chance to see, even for a fraction of a moment, our master's deepest compassion to safeguard life.

He takes great care not to step on ants or other insects while walking and, if he sees a worm toiling across the dry ground in the sun, he moves it into the shade on moist grass. When insects like mosquitoes, flies, ants, or spiders get into the room, he either chases them out of the window with his fan, or carefully puts them on to a dustpan and takes them outside, making sure that no part of their body is harmed.

One spring, the spindle trees by the master's residence became heavily infested with insects. He forbade us from using pesticides, saying that "I do not see my body, worms, or insects as being that much different from each other. The dignity and sanctity of life is the same, whether human or animal, small or large," and he asked us to pick up every one of the thousands of insects with wooden chopsticks, put them into a bottle and move them elsewhere.

There is a small pond in the monastery inhabited by a few frogs. Because the eggs they lay in spring attract snakes, we move them to a nearby reservoir. One day, a practitioner was scooping out the eggs to a bucket with a plastic bowl. When the eggs became stuck to the bowl, she repeatedly struck the bowl against the bucket to make them fall out. Wouldn't the eggs be startled if you hit hard like that, the master said when he saw this, and asked her to do it gently.

Once, on his way to a Dharma meeting, the master hurriedly asked the practitioner who was driving to pull over. He had never asked us to stop on the shoulder of an expressway before as it is dangerous, so thinking it strange, the practitioner stopped the car. As he switched on the emergency lights, he saw a grasshopper on the driver's side window. When he returned to the car after moving it to a safe place, the master said, "The grasshopper was holding on to the window with all its might to avoid falling from the car. How frightening and exhausting it must have been. Its legs were shaking so badly. Were you not able to see that?" The practitioner was lost for words, and could only lower his head in silence.

A practitioner once found a spider by the entrance to the master's room and, endeavoring to practice his teaching, she gently put it on to the dustpan to take it outside. But just as she was about to leave, the master said that if she left it out in the middle of the cold winter, it would freeze to death. He therefore told her to leave it in the room to let its life run its course, but put it in the far corner so that it would not be stepped on by people.

The practitioner realized how foolish she had been. Out of compassion to save and protect life, the master was moving worms, spiders, and insects to a place where they could live well, but to take the spider outside in the middle of winter was to simply mimic his actions without comprehending the true, underlying intention. She repented how she had interpreted and practiced his teachings in her own way.

Master Kim's compassion towards life applies equally, whether small or big, dangerous or harmless. During summer, snakes appear in the monastery as we are surrounded by mountains and fields and, because they can bite, he tells us to move them deep into the mountains where people do not visit. When moving a snake, he tells us to catch it in a net and not in a bag so that air can circulate easily, and when we occasionally delay moving it because we are occupied with something else, he asks us to release it in the mountains as soon as we can, saying how stifling it must be inside the net.

In the monastery, there is a maidenhair tree that stands eight to nine meters tall. When its leaves turn gold in fall, it is very beautiful to look at. Several years ago, we planted bamboo around the perimeter of the monastery, and the shoots grew quickly and soon spread to the maidenhair. Now densely surrounded by the bamboo trees, the maidenhair fell sick. Even though we walked past it several times a day, in our indifference we didn't realize how feeble it had become. But when the master saw this, he told us to immediately organize the bamboo trees nearby and install a hard barrier around it so that their roots could not spread towards the maidenhair. He then scolded our indifference, asking if we had never heard its agonizing cries even though we walked past it every day.

Several years ago, as he was leaving for a two-day trip to give Dharma lectures in Seoul, seeing how they were parched in the drought the master told us to thoroughly water the bamboo trees that had been planted as a fence around his residence. But this slipped our mind and we forgot to water them. As soon as he came back from the Dharma meeting, our master inspected the spot, and he was quite dismayed to see that we hadn't watered them. "Whether a human or a plant, without water, the suffering of thirst is the same. What if the bamboo trees had died? You cannot hope to achieve your goals in life when you don't look after the lives of others," and he made us water them straight away.

One day, I found a sunny spot to dry the laundry, and put a brick at the foot of the clothing rack to support it against the wind. I took away the clothes when they had dried, and left the brick and the rack where they were. When the master saw this, he said that there was a spot of grass under the brick. Pressed under the brick's weight and unable to receive sunlight, the grass would soon wilt and die, so he asked me to move the brick to a grassless spot.

Seeing how his tender care for life extends not only to humans or animals but even to a tree or a blade of grass, we come to repent how selfish, uncompassionate, and indifferent we are to other forms of life, even though we call ourselves spiritual practitioners. We also realize that one who cultivates the mind must practice compassion and the Bodhisattva Mind towards the whole world, and truly carry out the Bodhisattva Act with every step.

LIKE THE BAMBOO TREES
STANDING TALL TO THE SKY

Master Kim always ensures that any object or task is in its most needed place and in its most proper position. He shows the same compassion to all living beings and cultivates them by straightening what is uneven, cleaning what is dirty, organizing what is disorderly, by giving water when thirsty and nourishment when hungry. It is the same with the practitioners.

With personal examples, he shows us that the most rewarding life is one spent purifying the mind and planting merit. He tailors Dharma lectures to our individual circumstances and Dharma-hits us to take us forward. He is more pleased than anyone else if we make even a little progress or positive change in our practice. In any given circumstance, he imparts his wisdom to make us reflect and grow in maturity, and points out what we each need to change and surrender.

To ensure that the minds of practitioners do not wander away from the Buddha's monastery, our master planted lots of bamboo trees that grow tall quickly to act as a physical enclosure around the monastery.

One day, he called a practitioner to his side, and said that they should make a support for the bamboo together, for the trees were now leaning sideways as they had only recently been planted.

From right to left, from one end of the fence to the other, they pushed the leaning trees to make them upright again and, after hammering the support into the ground, they tied them to the support with rubber bands so that the young bamboo shoots could stand tall towards the sky.

They had been tying the bands for a while when the master spoke. "How is your mind? Isn't your mind leaning sideways like these young bamboo trees?"

Having only recently joined the monastery, the practitioner still had much on her mind. When she replied, "Yes, it seems to be leaning sideways." The master said, "Then straighten it up like these ones."

When she heard these words, besides the bamboo shoots that were now firmly tied to the support and standing upright towards the sky, to their right and left, she saw other bamboo trees that were leaning sideways and pointing in random directions. The master's words became a sturdy support for her to re-awaken her faith, and a foundation upon which to make her mind stand tall and upright.

PRACTICE THAT FLOWS LIKE WATER

One summer, the day after it had poured with rain, I was washing the farming tools I had used the day before in the mountain drain. Master Kim, who was watching from close by, saw how small and large stones inside the drain were obstructing the flow of water, and asked me to pull them out.

When all the stones had been cleared out, water gushed forth with a roar. The master then spoke. "How's the water? Isn't it flowing much better than before? You need to see others as Buddha. Then your practice will flow well like this water."

It was a Dharma lecture he gave knowing how my mind was full of dislike and hatred at the time, unable to surrender my discomfort towards a particular person.

One day, the master telephoned early in the morning and asked all of a sudden, "Today is the National Tree Planting day, so aren't you planting any trees?" We had recently planted some cornelian cherries at the monastery and, to the practitioner who was wondering if we were supposed to have planted anything else, the master spoke again.

"You need to plant a tree of reverence, a tree of devotion in your mind."

LEARNING FROM NATURE

From the clear, blue skies to the white, drifting clouds, from the murmurs of rivers to the fragrance of apricot blossom and even a stone on the grassland, Master Kim finds materials for his Dharma lectures in living examples from nature, and appropriately tailors them to our circumstances.

When young practitioners first enter the monastery and quarrel with their uncultivated minds, he gives the Dharma lecture of pebbles.

"The pebbles by the beach or river were rough stones at first, but after they clashed and hit against each other for a long time, they became round and smooth. Things are tough because rough and unpolished minds clash but, if you cultivate those minds as you endure, tolerate, and suffer, your mind will become gentle and smooth like the pebbles."

When a practitioner is going through a difficult period, weary in body and mind, he gives the following Dharma lecture.

"Look at those bamboo trees. Though their insides are empty, they stand tall and upright because they have joints in between their segments throughout. Like the joints in the bamboo trees, you grow stronger and healthier as you experience and overcome difficulties in life. Those who try to serve Buddha should be healthier in the mind."

Master Kim has published four books to date, which are *Polishing the Diamond, Enlightening the Mind* (1989), *Non-Dwelling, Exert the Mind* (1992), *Surrender That Mind* (1995) and *The Way to Cultivate the Mind* (1998). Of these, *The Way to Cultivate the Mind* is in the form of a small booklet. With donations from the lay followers of army Buddhist chaplain Kim Ung in the Korean armed forces and a small contribution from the Diamond Sutra Recitation Group, since its first publication in 1998, over 1.5 million copies have been printed to date and the booklet is distributed free of charge to the soldiers in military service.

But there have been instances where people copied our master's books verbatim, added their name on the front-cover, and handed them out, or published certain extracts in the media as if they were their own work. When he learned of this, our master would not say anything. But we couldn't just sit by and watch it happen, so when we contacted those people, most apologized and promised not to publish our master's work under the guise of their name again.

Three years ago, a certain Mr. "K" was also selling *The Way to Cultivate the Mind* in his Buddhist book shop after redesigning the cover to make himself appear as the author. We visited him to politely request that he stop selling our master's work without permission, but K insisted that it was a book he had written about his own spiritual practice and experiences. When we looked into the matter further, we discovered that we had forgotten to register the copyright, and in our omission K had made the registration in his name. We were left at a complete loss. Since K was now the copyright-holder, unless we took steps to correct this, we faced the prospect of not being able to publish our master's books under his own name.

Since K was adamant, we decided to take legal action to reclaim the copyright, and we went to explain the situation to the author himself, our master. However, he then began to ask us questions that we didn't expect.

"What does Mr. K do?"

"How is his store doing?"

"So if we take legal action against him, what will happen to him?"

When we explained that he would pay a fine, our master's worries began.

"I'm not so sure if he could afford to pay the fine. How much could he possibly earn by running a Buddhist book store? Is there a way to make sure that he doesn't pay the fine? See if we can pay it for him."

To an author, writing is said to be like giving birth, with all the pain of labor. In addition to the time and effort they pour in to publish the book, their writing is precious above all because it contains their soul. It is unpleasant enough that someone is using one's precious work without permission but, in the case of K, he had even registered the copyright in his name. Yet, without a modicum of discomfort, the master was concerned for his welfare, requesting us to make sure that no harm would come to him. Seeing him thus brought the words of Gandhi to my mind: "The truly noble know all men as one, and return with gladness good for evil done." I can only fold my hands and bow to that noble place of his where there is no "I" or "other," but all are as one.

When the court ruled on the issue and we successfully reclaimed the copyright, as per our master's wish, we immediately dropped the charges so that K would not suffer any financial loss.

Master Kim always thinks of others' problems as his own, and he can never bring himself to simply let them pass by. We achieve self-sufficiency at the monastery by making and selling traditional Korean foods and, as part of the ingredients we buy high quality sea salt produced in the county of Sinan and traditional *jugyeom* (bamboo salt) which is known for its many health benefits. But several years ago, the owner of the bamboo salt works contacted us to say that he was closing down because making bamboo salt was too arduous and attracted few workers. The master found it extremely regrettable that he was going to stop, and asked me to pass on several messages to encourage him to continue.

"A very long time ago, an enlightened master realized that when the world is coming to an end, the environment will be polluted and many diseases will appear. The master agonized over how to save many people, and so created the *jugyeom*. So making jugyeom is a good vocation that brings benefit to others, and persevering with it will help him too."

We could easily have found other suppliers if the owner no longer made the salt, but the master repeatedly asked us to persuade him to continue, saying that even though making bamboo salt is arduous, it was his way of benefiting people. Also, when work is hard and tiring, rather than thinking about quitting, he said that the healthy, wise mindset is to improve one's health so that the workload becomes manageable, and he told us to put the owner in touch with a trader of red ginseng so that he could look after his health with good medicine. The owner of the salt business still makes bamboo salt to this day.

After completing his spiritual practice of seven years and six months, since he turned thirty three and to this day, as I look back, I believe this is how his mindset has always been for the forty years that he has led the Diamond Sutra Recitation Group. As Master Kim nurtured the practice of his practitioners, nourished the practice of the members of the Diamond Sutra Recitation Group, prayed for the country and its people, prayed for the deliverance of souls who died defending their country, prayed for the deliverance of anguished souls unable to depart, and prayed for all living beings, there was never a life he could call his own.

There may have been scolding or admonition out of concern for his students, but I have never seen him blame or speak badly of others. Taking the responsibility for everything on to his own shoulders, he gives boundless love and unceasing forgiveness even to those who mean him harm. His noble and pure love for people—love which no one could stop him from bestowing on others, and one which even he calls his "illness"—it is something that transcends our respect and amazement and, in our inadequate eyes, often comprehension itself.

Persevering through the cold winter with a single coal-briquette a day, living in his tiny, moldy room with paltry meals that often made him ill, as he distanced his whole life from comfort and wealth while living in thrift and frugality, he established eight monasteries. He registered all the monasteries under a non-profit corporation, and drew up its articles so that once the group dissolves, all its assets will revert to the state. Even as one who supervises the spiritual practice of fifteen monasteries and their members, and who has printed five hundred thousand Diamond Sutras and distributed seven hundred thousand books on Korean history and culture throughout the world, he still refers to himself thus: "There are two types of worthless *gam* (persimmon) in the world. One is *Ttaeng-gam* (unripe persimmon), and the other is *yeong-gam* (petty old man). I am the latter, an ordinary yeong-gam living in the distant countryside."

Taking joy in seeing the eternal lives of many blossom with his sacrifice as the nourishing soil, his unrelenting reverence and compassion that never cease to repay gratitude and greatly benefit others—might this not be the true realization and practice of the Bodhisattva Path?

We again reflect upon his words, that the path of one who cultivates the mind is to practice the Bodhisattva Mind, Bodhisattva Act, and the Bodhisattva Path.

Glossary

Sanskrit: (Skt); Korean: (Kor)

Amitabha Buddha. The Buddha who rules over Sukhavati, the Western Pure Land. In the Korean Buddhist tradition, practitioners who wish to be born in the Pure Land recite his praise, *Namo Amitabha Buddha.*

Ananda. One of Shakyamuni Buddha's first and foremost disciples. He was the cousin of the Buddha and became his personal attendant. He is known for his remarkable memory and is credited with being able to recite all of the Buddha's teachings.

Anathapindika's park. In life stories of Shakyamuni Buddha, the wealthy merchant Anathapindika figures as one of the Buddha's most generous patrons. He established a monastery at Jetavana Grove for the Buddha and his disciples. It was here that the early community of monks and nuns would spend the rainy season, and it was here that the Diamond Sutra was taught.

arhat (Skt). "Worthy one." A title of esteem and reverence for the senior disciples of the Buddha. More generally, a person who has completely purified their karmic hindrances and attained nirvana.

Ashoka. Ruler of the Maurya empire in northern India, who ruled from 272-236 B.C. He supported the spread of Buddhism throughout his empire.

Avalokiteshvara. One of the most important bodhisattvas in Mahayana Buddhism. He represents the compassionate activity of the Buddha. See also *Gwanse-eum Bosal.*

Bai Zhang (720-814). Chinese Chan master of the Tang Dynasty.

360

bodhi (Skt). The wisdom of enlightened consciousness.

Bodhidharma (5th-6th centuries). The first patriarch of the Chinese Chan (Zen) Buddhist tradition. He achieved enlightenment after facing a wall in continuous seated meditation for nine years.

bodhisattva (Skt). An enlightened being who postpones his or her enlightenment in order to deliver sentient beings from samsara.

bok (Kor). "Merit." The blessed fortune that stems from positive actions and is stored in one's mind, which is the primary cause of one's future happiness.

Buddha-eye. Enlightened vision that sees the past, present, future, and beyond of all things.

Cao Cao (2nd–3rd centuries). Military strongman who united North China near the end of the Han era through a series of bloody campaigns.

Chan. Chinese word for Zen.

Jang-gwe (Kor). A kneeling posture where one keeps the hips and back straight.

Cheoljong. A king of the Joseon Dynasty (1392—1910).

Jugyeom (Kor). Traditional Korean salt which is prepared by inserting sea salt into a thick bamboo stub and baking it repeatedly with pine firewood. Quality of the salt depends on the number of times it has been baked, and salt that has been baked nine times is considered to be the highest quality with significant medicinal properties.

Danjeon. Located one inch below the navel, it is considered to be the center of gravity and a source of spiritual energy in people. Also known as *dantian* in Chinese.

Dharma (Skt). Dharma with an upper case "D" refers to the teachings of Buddha. With a lower-case "d," dharma refers to any and all phenomena.

Dharma-hitting. An expedient way of purging the practitioner's karmic hindrance by means of hitting him or yelling at him. This can only be carried out by a truly enlightened master and must only be administered to a highly advanced disciple.

Dharma Lecture. A discourse for the purpose of instruction, often based on Buddhist Scripture or the words of Buddha. It is designed to make the audience realize and practice the teachings of Buddha.

Dharmakaya (Skt). A Buddha's truth body: the essence of Buddha that has no physical existence but is represented by pure radiance or wisdom that completely fills the universe.

Diamond Sutra. "*Vajracchedikā Prajñāpāramitā Sūtra*" (Skt). Records of a particular set of oral instructions given by Shakyamuni Buddha after 40 years of teaching, when his students were far advanced in their spiritual practice, and Shakyamuni Buddha's own enlightenment was at its most complete. Reading the Diamond Sutra aloud, as translated by Master Kumārajīva (A.D. 334–413), is one of the principal spiritual practices advocated by Master Kim.

Dipankara Buddha. The first of twenty-four Buddhas who taught the Buddhist path prior to Shakyamuni Buddha. In the Chinese Buddhist tradition, he is considered one of the "three Buddhas of past, present, and future," together with Shakyamuni Buddha and Tathagata Maitreya.

Five Desires and Pleasures. Pleasure gained from satisfying the five basic desires, which are cravings for wealth, sex, fame, delicious food and sleep.

good roots. The fundamental qualities in sentient beings which will cause them to do good deeds.

Gu-eop. Literally meaning 'mouth-sin,' it refers to sins committed with the mouth. Contrasted with *Sim-eop* (mental sin) and *Sin-eop* (physical sin).

Haein-sa. One of the three most famous Buddhist temples in Korea. This temple represents the Dharma of the Three Jewels.

Hakuin (1689–1769). One of the foremost Zen masters of Japan. He revitalized the Rinzai school of Japanese Buddhism by stressing the importance of sitting meditation and formalizing the teaching of koans—paradoxical riddles designed to lead students to an experience of enlightenment.

Han Shan (7th century). A famous Tang Dynasty poet who lived on Mount Han Shan (Cold Mountain) and is known for his unorthodox ways.

Han Yu (768–824). Chinese Confucian poet of the Tang Dynasty.

Hinayana (Skt). "Lesser Vehicle." Originally a derogatory term coined by Mahayana Buddhists to refer to some other schools of early Buddhism. Master Kim uses the term in a more positive way to describe a strict adherence to monastic guidelines.

Hyecho (704~787 AD). A monk of the Silla period who traveled to India to study.

Jetavana Grove (also known as *Jeta Grove*). See *Anathapindika's park.*

Gantamsim (Kor). A mental state that craves material things.

karma (Skt). Any kind of physical, vocal, or mental action that imprints in the mind and subsequently becomes a cause that gives rise to certain consequences in the future. Karmic actions can be positive or negative and either intentional or unintentional.

karmic hindrance. A negative karma hindering the attainment of bodhi.

karmic retribution. The results of karmic actions.

karmic tie. A bond that exists between people in this or future lives (or has existed in past lives) that develops from karmic actions.

Kashyapa. See *Mahakashyapa.*

Kisaeng (Kor). A female entertainer and hostess at a drinking house.

Gwanse-eum Bosal (Kor). "Bodhisattva Avalokiteshvara." Invoking Avalokiteshvara by reciting *Namu Gwanse-eum Bosal* is a common Buddhist practice.

li. Traditional unit of measurement equaling about a third of a mile.

Mahayana (Skt). "Great Vehicle." A form of Buddhism that originated during the first centuries of the common era in India and subsequently spread throughout Asia. It stresses the importance of compassion and the innate potential for all beings to reach enlightenment.

Mahakashyapa. One of the ten great disciples of Shakyamuni Buddha. He was renowned for his asceticism and moral discipline.

Manjushri. The bodhisattva who embodies the enlightened wisdom of Buddhahood.

mantra (Skt). Words of power that one chants during meditation or worship.

Maudgalyayana. One of Buddha's disciples who was well known for his magical abilities.

Meju (Kor). Dried fermented soybean paste pressed into a square block. It serves as the basic ingredient for some of the key condiments in Korean cuisine, such as *Dwenjang* and *Ganjang.*

Mireukjon Yeoraebul (Kor). "Tathagata Maitreya." Reciting the name of the future Buddha, Maitreya, is one of the principal spiritual practices advocated by Master Kim.

Naong (1320–1376). A renowned master of the Koryo Dynasty (937-1392).

nirvana (Skt). The ultimate state of enlightenment realized and subsequently taught by Shakyamuni Buddha.

Nongae. A patriotic Korean woman who sacrificed herself to kill the general of an invading Japanese force in the 16th century.

barwon (Kor). An invocation of a prayer, vow, or selfless wish.

bosallim (Kor). Literally meaning "bodhisattva," in Korean this term is also used to refer to any female lay follower.

Prajnaparamita (Skt). "The Perfection of Wisdom." A popular class of Mahayana Buddhist scriptures that includes the Diamond Sutra.

pratyeka buddha (Skt). A class of Hinayana practitioners who achieve Buddhahood without a teacher.

samadhi (Skt). A meditative state that is characterized by calm, stability, and the absence of distraction.

samsara (Skt). The cycle of birth, death, and rebirth characterized by suffering and discontent.

Sangha (Skt). The community of Buddhist practitioners. Also, the third of the Three Jewels.

Shakyamuni Buddha. "Sage of the Shakya clan." The historical Buddha; the Buddha of the present age.

Shariputra. One of Shakyamuni Buddha's disciples, renowned for his wisdom.

Shi De (7th century). A Tang Dynasty poet and friend of Han Shan.

Shravasti. The region of India in which Anathapindika's park was located.

Siddhartha Shakyamuni. The personal name of Shakyamuni Buddha.

Silla. An era of Korean history (57 B.C.–A.D. 935) in which the country was unified and Buddhism flourished.

Sim-eop. Literally meaning *"mind-sin,"* it refers to sins committed with the mind such as hating and judging others. All sins originate as *sim-eop.* Contrasted with *Gu-eop* (verbal sin) and *Sin-eop* (physical sin).

Sin-eop. Literally meaning "body-sin," it refers to sins committed with the body. Contrasted with *Sim-eop* (mental sin) and *Gu-eop* (verbal sin).

Sin Saimdang (1504~1551) A woman of the Joseon Dynasty who became a symbol of ideal motherhood in Korea.

Songgwang-sa. One of the three most famous Buddhist temples in Korea. This temple represents the Sangha of the Three Jewels.

storehouse consciousness. According to the Yogacara system of Buddhist philosophy, this is the last of eight types of consciousness that make up the psychology of an individual. Experiences of past karmic activity are imprinted upon it, until the karmic effects of such experiences manifest in future lives.

Subhuti. One of Shakyamuni Buddha's disciples. He is the principal interlocutor in the Diamond Sutra.

surrender. The key part of the Diamond Sutra is when Subhuti asks Shakyamuni Buddha "how do we *make* the mind *surrender.*" The method of making the mind surrender, as realized by Master Baek and taught by Master Kim in this book, is to offer up to Buddha our thought, feeling, karmic hindrance and any phenomenon of the mind by reciting *Mireukjon Yeoraebul* on that thought, feeling, karmic hindrance, and phenomenon the moment we sense it and see it, just as it surfaces from the depths of the mind. While the Korean and Chinese use the original verb "make surrender," in the English translation, it is shortened to "surrender" for the sake of simplicity.

sutra (Skt). Any scripture that contains the teachings of Shakyamuni Buddha.

Dae An (571~644 AD). A renowned master who lived during the Silla period (57 B.C.–A.D. 935). He is known as Wonhyo's teacher.

Tai Dian. A Chan master of the Tang Dynasty.

tamsim (Kor). Greed.

darae (Kor). A type of fruit found in Korea that ripens in spring.

Dangun (2333 B.C.~). The founder of Korea who established the nation of Ancient Joseon in 2333 B.C. around Liaodong, Manchuria, and the Korean Peninsula. His reign marks the beginning of the Korean nation.

Tathagata (Skt). "Thus gone." One of the ten epithets of a Buddha.

Tathagata Maitreya. The title of the future Buddha who is to succeed Shakyamuni Buddha and deliver sentient beings from samsara. See also *Mireukjon Yeoraebul.*

Three Jewels. Buddha, Dharma, and Sangha. The three foundations of Buddhist life and practice.

Eumtamsim (Kor). Lust for somebody.

Upali. One of the ten great disciples of Shakyamuni Buddha. He was renowned for his monastic discipline.

Vimalakirti. The central character in the *Vimalakirtinirdesha Sutra.* He is a lay householder who nonetheless leads the life of a bodhisattva and is renowned for his wisdom.

Vulture Peak. A mountain near the central Indian city of Rajagriha where the Buddha gave many teachings.

Wisdom-eye. A spiritual eye that perceives through bright wisdom, transcending the time and space.

won (Kor). A wish, prayer, or vow.

Wonhyo (617~686 AD). A Korean Buddhist master who developed an indigenous form of Buddhism in Korea. Following his enlightenment on his way to China, he returned to Korea to write nearly two hundred commentaries on Mahayana sutras. He is renowned for his iconoclastic lifestyle and has become an inspirational symbol for Buddhism in Korea as a whole.

Yashodara. The wife of Shakyamuni Buddha prior to his renunciation.

Zhao Zhou (778~897 AD). Great Chan master of the Tang Dynasty.

Polishing the Diamond Enlightening the Mind
Reflections of a Korean Buddhist Master

Yong Hwa Publications
1269 Seonggok-ri, Heunghae-eup, Pohang
Phone: (+82) 54-261-2231

This book, first published by Wisdom Publications (Boston, USA) in 1999, is republished with the author's additions and emendations by Yong Hwa Publications (Pohang, Korea) in 2013.

Translated from the Korean by Han Yoon Sang, Chang Hang Jin
Korean text on cover: *Mireukjon Yeoraebul*

ISBN 978-89-969357-6-6 03220

Printed in Korea

이 도서의 국립중앙도서관 출판시도서목록(CIP)은
서지정보유통지원시스템 홈페이지(http://seoji.nl.go.kr)와
국가자료공동목록시스템(http://www.nl.go.kr/kolisnet)에서
이용하실 수 있습니다. (CIP제어번호: CIP2013014443)